PUFFIN BOOKS

Edited by Eleanor Graham.

PS136

SIX GREAT ENGLISHMEN

The six great men, Drake, Marlborough, Nelson, Keats, Dr Johnson, and Winston Churchill, are well chosen and wonderfully well presented. There is a delightful sense of perspective in the tel ng, and the sure touch of a man of experience and judgement, who understands very wel how to interest the young, writing of things that have rested a long time in his mind. 'What makes greatness?' he asks, and answers briefly – 'being on the side of life'. Plenty of men have had power and influence and used it on the other side, in destruction, and tyranny, with hatred and cynicism, but these chosen six loved life and went out to meet it gallantly, with relish, not caring for themselves: and they are heartening company.

SIX
GREAT ENGLISHMEN

Drake

Dr Johnson

Nelson

Marlborough

Keats

Churchill

AUBREY DE SÉLINCOURT

PENGUIN BOOKS

Penguin Books Ltd, Harmondsworth, Middlesex
U.S.A.: Penguin Books Inc., 3300 Clipper Mill Road, Baltimore 11, Md
AUSTRALIA: Penguin Books Pty Ltd, 762 Whitehorse Road,
Mitcham, Victoria

—

First published by Hamish Hamilton 1953
Published in Puffin Books 1960

Made and printed in Great Britain
by Hunt, Barnard & Co, Ltd,
Aylesbury

CONTENTS

*

ACKNOWLEDGEMENTS

AND SOME SUGGESTIONS FOR FURTHER READING

Apart from standard works, I have been indebted chiefly to the following books:

Sir Francis Drake, by James A. Williamson.
Nelson, by Carola Oman.
Marlborough: his Life and Times, by the Rt Hon. Winston S. Churchill.
Mr Churchill: a Portrait, by Philip Guedalla.

In addition to the books above mentioned, the following are recommended for further reading:

FOR DRAKE: J. A. Froude's *England's Forgotten Worthies* (a stimulating essay in Froude's *Short Studies on Great Subjects*, available in Everyman edition). Hakluyt's *Voyages*. The relevant parts of this great work are indispensable, as contemporary and first-hand accounts.

FOR MARLBOROUGH: The biographies are numerous, but have all been superseded by Churchill's *Marlborough: his Life and Times*. Of the older biographies, the most useful is Archdeacon Coxe's *Memoirs of John, Duke of Marlborough* (1820). For background study of the period, necessary books are Prof. R. C. Trevelyan's *England under Queen Anne* (3 vols.).

FOR NELSON: Clennell Wilkinson's *Nelson* (a brilliant, short biography). For general pictures of life at sea in Nelson's day, the novels of Capt. Marryat are valuable and highly entertaining. For the same purpose C. S. Forester's *Hornblower* stories are both accurate and exciting.

FOR JOHNSON: The two indispensable books are Boswell's *Life of Johnson* and *A Tour to the Hebrides*. Apart from Johnson's own writings, *Johnson's England*, ed. Turberville (recently reissued by the Oxford University Press), is recommended as

ACKNOWLEDGEMENTS

the most useful and agreeable of the countless books which have been written upon Johnson and his times.

FOR KEATS: The best of the many biographies is still Sidney Colvin's *John Keats* (1917). Very useful for facts is Amy Lowell's *John Keats*, a more recent book (1925). A brilliant interpretative study is J. Middleton Murry's *Keats and Shakespeare*. For contemporary notices, Leigh Hunt's *Autobiography* should be consulted, and Charles Cowden Clarke's *Reminiscences of Writers* (though this is hard to come by). Colvin's edition of the *Letters* is as good as any, though it omits many of those written to Fanny Brawne.

FOR CHURCHILL: Sir Winston Churchill's own works, especially *My Early Life* and *Lord Randolph Churchill: a Biography*.

FOREWORD

Greatness is not an easy thing to define, but it is just as well that when we speak of it, as we very often do, we should be as clear as possible about what we mean. Can one, for instance, be a great sailor, or a great soldier, or a great poet – or a great anything else – without being a great man? Personally, I think that one can. To be a great man requires a certain quality over and above pre-eminent ability in a particular line of business.

Believing this, I have chosen the six people who are described in this book, because it seems to me that they all possessed, or possess, this quality, and the longer I have lived with them in imagination, while reading and writing about them, the surer I have become of the nature of the thing which binds them together and makes them, in spite of their differences, akin to one another.

To put it briefly, these men are *on the side of life*. There have been men of immense power and influence in the world (recent examples in Europe will readily occur to mind) who have not been on the side of life, but on the side of death – the oppressors and destroyers, the cynics, the doubters, the haters. These are not to be admitted into the company of the great, even though their power should change the world. On the contrary, the six men in this book, like all others who belong to their fellowship, are on the side of life because they have loved it, and have gone out to meet it gallantly and with relish, not caring about their own skins. They have looked outward, and, if they have encountered pain or disappointment – well, that is in the nature of this difficult, mysterious, but nevertheless beautiful world. For this reason they and their like are heartening company; and many of us need heartening today, when to our eager questions so many dusty answers are given.

I have not tried in these sketches to find new facts, or to upset established judgements. But no two pairs of eyes, when they have looked long and closely at an object, will see it quite the same; and any novelty in my portraits will be due to the fact that the eyes were mine, and not somebody else's. I hesitated at first to include the portrait of a contemporary, because of the obvious difficulties it involves; but it seemed wrong to leave out the one man of our own times who so plainly belongs to the same order of life as the other five in my book. I have ventured, therefore, to include Sir Winston Churchill. Some may be disappointed that I have said so little about the climax of Sir Winston's career: of his part, that is, in the war against Nazi Germany. My excuse is that limits of space made adequate treatment of it impossible. In any case, the last war is still fresh in our minds, and it seemed to me better to confine myself to the attempt to describe, through the less familiar incidents of Sir Winston's earlier life, the quality of mind and spirit which enabled him to perform, when the time came, the greatest of his services to England.

Niton, I.W.
January 1953

Drake

MEN are quarrelsome creatures, and much given to using their divine gift of reason for the purpose of putting their quarrels upon a satisfactory basis. It is an old game, and a good one; for often enough in the playing of it they lay so strong a spell upon their fancy that a cause which might make the angels laugh, or weep, becomes a glory and a high romance.

One of the most persistent and satisfactory bases for quarrelling in human history has been difference of religion: Turk and Jew, Christian and infidel, Catholic and Protestant, each to the other a 'man who believes the wrong thing' – in fact a miscreant, and therefore wicked. Religion binds men together for many objects besides the common worship of God – and sets them at their neighbours' throats.

When Elizabeth I came to the throne in 1558, England was a small country with a population about half as big as that of present-day London; it was still torn by religious feuds, and so poor that the Queen, whose income was less than half a million a year, was unable to maintain a regular army, or even a navy except the smallest. The towns were ill-built, crowded, and pestilent; in the countryside and villages there was insufficient work and much destitution; beggars and tramps were a menace to domestic peace; periodical plagues exacted a heavy toll of life; manners were brutal and savage – men hanged for the pettiest thefts, and for grave crimes disembowelled before death to provide a spectacle for their fellows. The arts were half-asleep: no poet of consequence had yet appeared since Chaucer's death a century and a half before. Nevertheless, in the collective spirit of the men and women of England a powder-train had somehow been lighted, which before the reign was over was to explode into a blaze of unprecedented splendour; England was finally to realize herself as a nation and to see clear before her the path which she must follow, and did follow for nearly three hundred and fifty years, to pre-eminence amongst the nations of the world, in power, in commerce, and in poetry – the noblest of the arts and itself the expression of the flaming life of the people for whose delight it was written.

What struck the spark to kindle the powder-train – what produced that extraordinary upsurge of the human spirit which marks the first Elizabethan age – nobody can know. Such things do happen, thanks to the restless and indomitable spirit of men. What sustained it, what forms it took in the imaginations of the men then living, working, and adventuring, it is easier to say: the chief of them was the image of an England yet young asserting her liberty to enjoy in her own way the inexhaustible riches of the world, material and spiritual, against the old, oppressive, and mighty power of Catholic and feudal Spain. In the work of winning this liberty no class of men were more directly engaged than the English seamen, already for centuries in the front rank for their knowledge of the narrow seas, but then for the first time adventuring across the oceans of the world. Amongst the seamen two names have always been pre-eminent: John Hawkins and Francis Drake – the former for his invaluable administrative achievements and steady vision of the essential bases of naval strategy and power, the latter for a series of brilliantly improvised dramatic strokes in a setting of wild adventure and romance, which has caught and held the imagination of our poetic race more firmly than anything else of the sort since Odysseus put to sea from Tenedos after the capture of Troy.

Drake was born about 1540, perhaps a year or two later, near Tavistock in Devon. Ships and the sea were familiar to him from earliest childhood; for his father had been a sailor before he took to farming, and doubtless talked to his boy of the old days which no sailor can forget. Then, when he was seven or eight years old, the family, which was strongly Protestant in religion, was forced by the rising of the peasants against the new form of Church service introduced by Cranmer, to leave the Devonshire farm and take refuge elsewhere. They moved to Gillingham in Kent, on the river Medway, where just about this time the new dockyard, to be known as the Chatham dockyard, was established by the Council of King Edward VI. Here they lived in an old condemned ship, a kind of home in which the boy Francis and his brothers (two of whom were later to sail with him and meet an early death) no doubt took more pleasure than his mother did.

What Drake did and dreamed during his passionate and imperious boyhood can only be guessed; for there is no record. But it is not hard to guess, his surroundings being what they were. As a young man he went to sea in a coasting vessel, which was left to him by her owner when he died. In her he learned his first lessons in seamanship and command, the indispensable foundation of his technical knowledge; for a man who can sail a ship on our difficult and dangerous coasts, in and out of their rivers and havens, ill-marked and ill-charted as they were in those days, can sail her without fear anywhere in the world. But though Drake's trading trips from port to port on the English coasts occupied his time for a few years, they hardly occupied his thoughts: those were set upon the oceans and the lands beyond them, the Indies and the Spanish Main, the spice islands of the East, and Peru on the Pacific coast, where no English ship had yet sailed.

His opportunity soon came. Hawkins, who was a distant cousin of Drake's and older by some nine or ten years, had opened a trade with the Spanish colonies in the West Indies. Drake, therefore, sold his coaster and offered himself for service in the new venture. Hawkins was willing to accept him, and in 1566 he sailed as a junior officer under the command of John Lovell. The trade was in slaves – picked up along the African coast and shipped across the Atlantic to wretched labour and the only happiness of a swift and early death. It was a beastly trade; but there is little wisdom in growing hot about the beastliness of men, which takes different forms in different ages. It seems an inconsistency in a people whose lives were devoted to the pursuit of a newly realized freedom, to snatch at a share in the slave-trade; and indeed it was. To the sixteenth-century Englishman an African Negro was not a man at all; he was a commodity and a valuable one, and quick profits have seldom helped people to detect immorality in the means of winning them. In this the sixteenth century was not very different from any other – and indeed, so far as the slave-trade goes, it was to remain a reputable form of business for another two hundred years.

Lovell's expedition failed as a business venture, but it taught Drake how not to deal with the Spaniards even in peace, and by first opening to him the scene of many of his future triumphs, set him dreaming upon what was to come. The following year he was back upon the same coast – that strip some 300 miles long in the north-east corner of South America between Santa Marta and the Isthmus of Panama, so long known to history and romance as the Spanish Main – this time with Hawkins himself and in command of the bark *Judith*, 50 tons. Again the object of the voyage was to sell Negroes to the Spanish colonists, and, Hawkins being a better man than

Lovell, trade was brisk, until bad weather and Spanish treachery brought the expedition to disaster. There were six ships in the fleet, and one of them, the *Jesus*, had given trouble in a blow a week after leaving Plymouth on the outward passage. She had been built on the Baltic many years before, and her towering superstructures fore and aft made her a typical specimen of the old-fashioned naval architecture, which the genius of Drake and Hawkins was soon to render obsolete in all British ships. These superstructures caused fearful strain when the ship rolled heavily in bad weather, so that the fastenings were loosened and the seams opened. Hawkins got her across the Atlantic, but on the way home, as the fleet was making for the Florida channel, they were caught by another severe gale off the western end of Cuba. The *Jesus* again leaked like a sieve, and it seemed for a time as if she would have to be abandoned. But the weather improved, and Hawkins decided to risk entering the harbour of San Juan de Ulua – Vera Cruz – for a refit. This little port, which lay due east of the city of Mexico, of course belonged to Spain; but as England and Spain were then nominally at peace, all might have been well. The port consisted of a shallow bay, running inland about a quarter of a mile, and protected on the north – to seaward – by a low bank, or islet, of stones some two hundred yards long, with a navigable passage on either side. The fleet entered without difficulty – indeed, the people there took them for Spaniards, and were doubtless embarrassed when they realized their mistake. The Spanish plate-fleet, which called once a year to ship the treasure from the Mexican mines, was daily expected, and Hawkins at once took precautions both to protect his own ships and to put their presence in the foreign port upon a proper footing. He dispatched a messenger to Mexico, declaring his peaceable intentions and asking leave to buy stores and effect repairs without molestation, and at the same time landed guns on the stony islet to cover the entrance to the harbour.

Before his messenger could return from the capital, the Spanish plate-fleet arrived off the entrance – thirteen large ships. Hawkins knew that, having command of the island, he could keep them out, and, if he did so, that they would almost certainly be lost; for it was a dangerous coast, and the first northerly blow would pile them up on a lee shore. Moreover, he did not trust the Spanish commanders, and feared a treacherous attack if he let them in. But his trouble was that England was not at war with Spain, and he was well aware that, if he caused the loss of a couple of million pounds' worth of Spanish property, the consequences to himself, when he returned to England, would be grave – for still, and for a number of years yet, the main object of the Queen's policy was to preserve the nice balance of an uneasy peace. It was an awkward situation. Hawkins decided to 'abide' – as he put it – 'the jut of the uncertainty', and to let the Spaniards in. He was, of course, perfectly right; but one can fancy that Drake, young and inexperienced though he still was, lifted an eyebrow at his senior's caution.

With the Spaniards was Don Martin Enriquez, the viceroy of New Spain, and he and Hawkins at once entered into an agreement, binding each party to respect the other's needs. Three days later suspicious movements were observed both on board the Spaniards and on shore; arms were being shifted from ship to ship, guns trained to bear upon the island, and men were thought to have been smuggled during the night into a great hulk of 900 tons which was moored close alongside the English ship *Minion*. Hawkins sent a man to Don Martin to protest; and Don Martin, seeing that his plot was discovered, gave the signal for an immediate assault. The ships were packed like sardines in the little harbour, and the fight which ensued was savage and confused. Spanish soldiers poured aboard the *Minion*, where Hawkins himself narrowly escaped being stabbed by a Spanish nobleman whom he was entertaining to supper. The Englishmen on the island came under immediate fire from the Spanish guns, and Spanish troops from the mainland crossed over in boats and killed all who survived the gunfire. Three Spanish ships were sunk, and only two of the English – Drake's *Judith* and the *Minion* – succeeded in getting away. Drake made straight for England; Hawkins in the *Minion*, desperately overcrowded and short of victuals, followed a few days later. Half of his men he put ashore on the American coast; most of the remainder died on the voyage home. When the *Minion* brought up in Mount's Bay, the remnant of his ship's company were so weak from sickness and lack of food that a fresh crew had to be put aboard to bring her in to Plymouth.

Hawkins wrote his own account of this ugly episode. In it he accused Drake – though not by name – of deserting him. Two other accounts, written by two survivors from the party put ashore in the Bay of Mexico, are preserved in the great collection of *Voyages* edited by Hakluyt; in neither of them is there any suggestion of desertion. We shall never know. The precise nature of the complex motives which determine any action are hard enough to assess, even when it takes place before our eyes. It would have been unlike Drake to abandon a friend in distress; but he was never a good subordinate – he obeyed, usually for the best, his own inward *daemon*, which prompted the immediate stroke: and, even if he had stayed to bear Hawkins company, he could have done nothing to ease him.

For Drake, the fight at San Juan had consequences of the utmost importance. The treachery of Don Martin Enriquez he never forgot, and the effect of the first impact of it was to crystallize in his mind, once and for all, the shape which his life's work was to take. Driven as a child from his home by the Catholic enemy, he had seen in the impressionable years of his adolescence the burning of martyrs under Queen Mary; the huge and oppressive Catholic power threatened to engulf not only England, but the world; and now to cruelty and oppression was added treachery. England might maintain the precarious balance between uneasy peace and undeclared war, but henceforward Drake himself was dedicated to the destruction of the Spanish power whenever, and wherever, he could deal a blow. How far he succeeded is shown by the story of the Spanish rabble in Madrid, who, after the defeat of the Armada, mocked its admiral, Medina Sidonia, by shouting under his windows '*Viene el Draque*' – Drake is coming.

After San Juan de Ulua Drake was at home for a year. He married, and then was off to sea again. This time he was his own master. His ship was the *Swan*, 25 tons – no bigger than what many a yachtsman would sail today with one friend to help him. She was fitted out for him in Plymouth by Hawkins and his partner Sir William Winter – a fact which suggests that Hawkins's anger against Drake was already forgotten. The purpose of the voyage was to collect information to be used for a future stroke, and was authorized by the Queen. Drake's master-plan was already forming; Hawkins wholeheartedly supported it, and if it had been fully carried out, the power of Spain might have been effectively broken. The plan was grandly and simply designed. Spain was in herself a poor country, and she was able to maintain large fleets and large armies both at home and in the Netherlands only by means of the inexhaustible treasure which she drew from her colonial possessions across the Atlantic. Stop the flow of treasure and she would be crippled. Much of it came from the mines in Mexico, but by far the richest source was Peru, land of the ancient Incas, on the Pacific coast. From Peru the treasure was carried up the coast to Panama, taken across the isthmus on the backs of mules, and reshipped at the port of Nombre de Dios. On the whole isthmus – some three hundred miles in length – Panama, Nombre de Dios, and a little place between the two called Venta Cruces were the only Spanish settlements; the eastern half was occupied by the Cimaroons, slaves who had escaped from Spanish masters and their bitter enemies. If the two ports could be taken and held – or even Nombre de Dios only – the treasure route would be cut, and the strength of Spain drained away.

With sufficient men and ships, and proper equipment, this could no doubt have been done. But it would have been an act of war – and Spain and England were at peace. It was not for another ten or eleven years that the Queen finally consented to recognize the necessity of open war. Yet the peace was peace only in name, and nobody knew this better than the Queen. Again and again she was on the verge of open war, but the difficult and delicate balance was held. Elizabeth loved her seamen and admired them, as they loved and worshipped her, and any blow which they could deal the common enemy she welcomed with secret joy; but – they must do it on their own initiative, not upon orders from her. They must take the consequences of their own failure or success. They were gentlemen adventurers, not servants of the crown. If they robbed a Spanish ship, she must be able to pretend that it was a wilful and lawless act which she had been powerless to stop. She was not yet ready for war in name as well as in deed: she had not the money to finance it, apart from her passionate conviction that England needed peace, if it could possibly be kept. Spanish writers have called Drake a pirate – and some English writers too. The case against him is easy to make out upon a basis of mere logic: that a man, namely, who sacks the towns and plunders the ships of a friendly country, *is* a pirate. But logic here, as so often in human affairs, is a poor guide to truth, and its conclusion is directly contrary to the reality of the situation and the whole spirit of the time. Drake and his compeers, by their reckless and brilliant adventures and growing mastery of the oceans of the world, were serving England as truly and directly, within the circumstances of their age, as Nelson himself served her at Copenhagen and Trafalgar. That they were serving themselves at the same time, and growing rich on the wealth of Spain, is no less true. We need not blink the fact. Self-interest is the driving-force behind most of the deeds of men; but there are periods in history when circumstances and the temper of the time link it to larger issues and shed upon it a larger light, by which it is mysteriously transformed. When Hawkins, after the disaster at San Juan de Ulua, asked the Queen for permission to undertake a fresh expedition to repair his losses, he was offering himself as the servant of his country too; and when Drake returned rich from his voyage round the world, he had done more than any other single man in history to prove what England's future destiny must be. Man is a grasping and quarrelsome animal; but there are times – as Keats observed – when his quarrel has a grace in it, and love of adventure, and desire for gain, are lifted beyond themselves and merged into something that transcends them. The plunder and piracy of Elizabethan England were identified in the imaginations of men with an inspired crusade against the thumbscrew and the rack of the Spanish Inquisition. To understand them properly we must make the same effort of imagination ourselves.

During the time that Drake was on the coast with his little *Swan*, he picked up all the information he could from direct observation, from the friendly Cimaroons, and from any French adventurers he happened to meet;

then, with his plan growing to completion in his mind, he returned to Plymouth to consult Hawkins about ways and means for equipping an expedition on a larger scale. The following year – 1572 – he was off again with two ships: the *Swan*, as before, and the *Pasco*, 70 tons. Into these two small vessels he packed guns, military equipment, about seventy men and, in addition, three open boats – or pinnaces – each capable of holding from thirty to forty people. They were stowed in the holds in pieces, ready to be put together without loss of time when the occasion should arise. The crowding must have been frightful; and when one realizes that nothing was then known about the elementary laws of diet and hygiene, it is easy to see that, apart from the necessary risks of the sea and of battle, a man in those days had to be tough to survive an ocean voyage.

Drake's plan was to go straight for Nombre de Dios, the port of embarkation for the Peruvian treasure. Leaving the ships at an island anchorage off the Isthmus coast to the eastward, he put his force into the pinnaces and made for the town under cover of darkness. It was not yet dawn when the three boats entered the harbour; the place was asleep, and ill-guarded. Silently the men landed; a party under John Oxenham, a man, like Drake, of reckless gallantry as his subsequent adventures proved, was sent round to the further side of the town, and, on the signal from Drake's trumpeter, the two parties burst in simultaneously. The surprise was complete. There was one volley of musket-fire from the Spanish troops, and the garrison fled – but they had killed the trumpeter and shot Drake through the leg. Drake kept going. He ordered his brother John to break open the treasure house, while he himself held the centre of the town against a possible return of the Spanish troops. But he collapsed from loss of blood before John could succeed. The position was critical: it was near dawn, and the

Spaniards would rally when they found the enemy force so much smaller than they expected. There was nothing for it but retreat. Drake was carried back to the harbour, and the three boats slipped away.

The first attempt had failed; but there was soon to be a second – this time not upon the town, but directly upon a laden mule-train on its way from Panama. A few months were let go by, during which Drake cruised to the eastward, living well off the stores in Spanish ships which he captured; he even, with a sort of gay insolence, took his pinnaces into the harbour of Cartagena, the chief city of the Spanish Main. Then once more he landed on the Isthmus. This time he had the help of the Cimaroons, who acted as his guides through the wooded and mountainous country of the interior. On the crest of the central ridge the little party halted, close by a huge tree – the Cimaroons' watch-tower. The guides took Drake up, and from the top he saw to the southward, for the first time in his life, the distant shimmer of the Pacific. Then Oxenham went up and saw it too – and for one brief moment, the ambush of a mule-train from Panama must have seemed to both men a little thing. Soon they were down again; the march continued, and the trap was laid. The mule-train was heard approaching. All was ready – when a man in Drake's party let off his musket by mistake and gave the alarm.

Back they tramped to the coast, fifty miles or more through mountains and trackless forest, with nothing gained. But their spirits were high, and the third attempt was to succeed. Again, when the alarm had died down, the friendly Cimaroons consented to guide them, and this time they had an accession of strength in a party of Frenchmen off a French rover under the command of le Testu. Drake left some men to guard the pinnaces and once more the ambush was set. Unsuspecting, the mule-drivers and their Spanish guard approached along the single track. A volley of musketry and arrows, a shout, a brisk charge, and the train was captured. It was a rich prize, but not yet safely won; for they had to get the treasure to the coast and aboard the pinnaces before the Spaniards in Panama and Nombre de Dios could muster in strength and attack them. It was a tough task; each man with more than a man's load staggered through the wild country northwards towards the sea. When they arrived, worn out, they found the pinnaces gone. It was a desperate moment, but Drake was equal to it. The previous day it had been blowing hard from the westward and it was blowing still; he guessed at once that the pinnaces had been forced to run eastward for shelter. There was no time to lose; if he was to save his men, and the gold, he must make contact with them quickly – but how? On the instant he made his decision: felling some trees near the beach, he built a raft, launched her, and with a couple of companions aboard to help him, let her drive before the wind along the coast. In a few hours he saw the pinnaces struggling back to windward under sail. Running the raft ashore, he hailed them, and was taken aboard. Briefly, he told the crews about the captured treasure; then, all through the night, they fought their way with oars and sails back to the creek where the other men were waiting. All was still safe: the Spaniards were forestalled, and without loss of an hour the precious cargo was stowed in the pinnaces, transferred to the ship, and sail made for England.

Drake entered Plymouth Sound on a Sunday. Swiftly the news of his arrival spread through the town, and every house and every church was emptied, as men and women crowded to the waterside to greet him. His apprenticeship was over; he was now a famous man. He had demonstrated beyond all doubt what damage could be done to the pride and pocket of Spain by a small ship resolutely and skilfully handled.

It was natural, therefore, that four years later when the uneasy pulse of the relationship between the Queen and King Philip was once again quickening towards war, Drake should be the man chosen for special service of the utmost importance. On the advice of Sir Francis Walsingham, he was summoned to the Queen's presence. 'Drake,' she said, 'so it is that I would gladly be revenged on the King of Spain for divers injuries I have received.' The words must have been music in Drake's ears. Exactly what passed at this famous interview, the precise nature of the blow which Drake was authorized to strike at the power of Spain, is not known. A year before, Oxenham had sailed to the Isthmus of Panama, with Drake's full knowledge and support. Helped by the Cimaroons, he had left his ship somewhere on the north coast and marched inland with his men. Then, on a river bank, he had built a pinnace, launched her, and sailed into the Pacific. Making his base on an island off the coast, he proceeded to attack and plunder the ill-armed Spanish shipping coming up from the southward, until he had amassed a considerable treasure, which he hid on the mainland. The whole story of Oxenham's adventure – the march through the mountains, the building of the boat, the first touch of the water of the Pacific on an English keel – is as wild and stirring as any in history. The fact that it is so little remembered is a revealing comment on the tone and temper of the Elizabethan age. We cannot be sure what Oxenham's purpose was, beyond his treasure-hunting; but it is not impossible that before he sailed he had made with Drake the outline of some larger plan, in which the two men might later cooperate – perhaps the permanent holding of the Isthmus of Panama with the assistance of the Cimaroons. But whatever the plan was, Oxenham was caught by the Spaniards before it could unfold. The news of his capture had not reached England at the time of

Drake's interview with the Queen, and though it is unlikely that the Queen herself, who still hoped to keep the
peace in spite of her desire to be revenged on King Philip,
would have risked what would have amounted to a major
operation of war, the possibility of it may well have been
in Drake's mind. The official instructions she gave Drake
were innocent enough: he was to sail south and west
through the Magellan Straits in search of the Great
Southern Continent which then and until the time of
Captain Cook, two centuries later, was believed to exist –
the Terra Australis Incognita, a mythical land of plenty,
which England was to colonize. But Drake had his secret
instructions too – so secret that no other man in England
was to be told what they were. Above all, they had
to be kept from the Lord Treasurer, the cautious
Burghley.

By some means or other the secret came to the ears of
one other man – Thomas Doughty. Perhaps he was concealed in the room, as Burghley's spy, during the interview between Drake and the Queen – for though Burghley was loyal to England's honour, he would have gone
to any lengths to prevent a stroke which might precipi-
tate war. It is possible that Drake himself made Doughty
his confidant; for he loved and trusted him. It was a
strange friendship; the two men had met in Ireland not
long before, and no pair could have been more opposite –
Drake simple, imperious, passionate, ignorant of intrigue, contemptuous of treachery, and a born leader of
men; Doughty a self-seeker, courtly and polished, and
an adept in crooked ways to private ends. The sea itself
is not more mysterious than human affection and love.

The expedition fitted out at Plymouth – in the old
harbour of Sutton Pool – and sailed in November 1577.
Doughty accompanied it. There were five vessels in the
fleet, all small, even Drake's *Pelican* being not more than
about 150 tons. Somewhere in the Atlantic it became

apparent to Drake that trouble was brewing: Doughty was inciting men to mutiny. Drake put him under arrest. The passage was a slow one, with calms and baffling winds, and by the time the fleet was on the South American coast, the temper of both officers and men was as bad as it could be. Nerves were jumpy, loyalties divided: the most momentous voyage in English history was on the point of petering out, with nothing achieved. The ships entered the harbour of St Julian, a hundred miles north of the entrance to the Straits of Magellan. On a rock by the waterside stood the remains of a gibbet, on which nearly sixty years before the great Portuguese seaman had hanged a mutineer. It was a grim welcome. Drake knew that hesitation would be fatal. Doughty was brought to justice and tried for his life on a charge of mutiny. He admitted that he had communicated to Burghley the plan of the voyage. His subsequent work in sowing dissension amongst the ships' companies was evident and could not be denied. Drake called for a show of hands – *guilty* or *not guilty*. Almost every hand was raised – perhaps for fear of Drake, for he could be as terrible, when the need arose, as he was merciful to prisoners taken in war. The traitor Doughty died like a gentleman. After the manner of those days, when men felt less need to conceal their feelings than we do today, he took Communion with Drake at the hands of the ships' chaplain and dined with him on the best that that wild place could afford. Then, saying he was ready, he embraced his commander and 'in quiet sort' laid his head on the block.

The traitor was dead, but much of the effect of his work remained. The expedition was still far from unanimous; the gentlemen were idle and disaffected, the sailors unruly and jealous of their superiors. It was no fit company for a perilous enterprise. A month after Doughty's execution, Drake ordered everyone ashore. It was Sunday, and when all were assembled, Fletcher the chaplain offered to preach them a sermon; Drake, however, said no – he would preach the sermon himself. At once he proceeded to do so, and of all sermons ever preached it was the most immediately effective. 'Thus it is, my masters,' he said, 'that we are very far from our country and friends, and compassed in on every side with enemies; wherefore we must have these mutinies and discords that are grown amongst us redressed. Here is such controversy between the sailors and the gentlemen, and such stomaching between the gentlemen and sailors, that it doth even make me mad to hear it. But, my masters, I must have it left: I must have the gentleman to haul and draw with the mariner, and the mariner with the gentleman. What? Let us show ourselves all to be of one company, and not give occasion to the enemy to rejoice at our overthrow. I would know him that would refuse to set his hand to a rope.'

There was no refusal, and Drake – who by this startling demand had set on foot a practice which by Nelson's time was to develop into the identification of the sailing and fighting services in ships at sea – offered one of his ships to any malcontents who might choose to return to England rather than continue the voyage. None chose to accept the offer. Suddenly and without warning Drake informed his officers that every one of them was deprived of his command. Then, having revealed to them – what none of them yet knew – that he was out by the Queen's orders to harass the Spaniards in the Indies and the neighbourhood of Panama, he asked if they now would follow him of their own free will. There was not a single dissentient voice. 'And now,' he ended, 'let us consider what we have done: we have set together by the ears three mighty princes – her Majesty, and the Kings of Spain and Portugal; and if this voyage should not have good success, we should not only be a scorning or a scoffing-stock to our enemies, but also a great blot to our whole country for ever. And the like would never be attempted again.'

After that, there was no doubt who was master. Drake renamed his ship *Golden Hind*. The officers were restored to their commands; and the fleet of three (two had been broken up at St Julian) sailed southward. It was now August, and on the 21st the ships entered the Straits of Magellan, those gloomy waters

> wrack'd with perpetual storm
> Of whirlwind and dire hail,

where the williwaws sweep down from the mountains with hurricane force, and the mountains themselves, black and desolate, tower so high that 'three regions of cloud' lie on their slopes. Drake's fleet made a record passage through the Straits: by 6 September his ships were clear of Cape Pillar and in the Pacific. This sixteen-day passage is an interesting and remarkable achievement. At the end of last century Joshua Slocum, in his weatherly little sloop *Spray*, took nearly a week longer to get through, a fact which proves that the Elizabethan ships, so clumsy and leewardly-looking to modern eyes, were much more capable of windward work than is usually supposed. They must, moreover, have been superbly handled, for their rig – course with bonnets on fore and main; topsails over; a lateen mizzen; and for fair winds and fine weather, a square water-sail under the bowsprit – was the most unhandy and awkward that can be imagined. But they did sail – and certainly made rings round those floating pantechnicons, the Spanish treasure galleons.

The Pacific, when Drake entered it for the first time in his life, belied its name, as it too frequently does. A heavy northerly gale scattered the fleet and drove it far to the southward. One ship – *Marigold* – was lost with all hands;

another, under the command of John Winter, failed to regain contact and returned to England. Drake in *Golden Hind* was henceforward alone.

An English ship on the Pacific coast was the last thing the Spaniards expected. In the Caribbean they were used to trouble, but the coast of Chile and Peru had hitherto been their own. Their ports were guarded lightly or not at all; none of their ships was armed – and the cargoes they carried were of silver, jewels, and gold. For Drake it was a rich hunting-ground, and he made full use of his opportunities. It was on this coast that he first learnt that Oxenham had been taken (he was hanged a year later by the Spaniards in Lima) and his men killed, so whether or not he had hoped to join him in holding the Isthmus of Panama, he was no longer able to do so. But there were other blows he could strike at the power and the pride of Spain, though none, perhaps, so immediately decisive. The Spanish ships and ports were at his mercy; a master of surprise attack, he took what he wanted with hardly the loss of a man, and little by little the ballast of the *Golden Hind* was changed to precious metal instead of iron and stone. One of his raids has an air of gaiety about it which is very pleasant: on leaving Valparaiso far from empty-handed, he put in at a little port called Tarapaza. Here his men found a Spaniard asleep on the beach with a pile of silver bars beside him: 'We took the silver,' says the old chronicler, 'and left the man.'

But the making of the voyage was the capture of the great ship *Cacafuego* (Spitfire), of which Drake had news in Lima, the port of Peru. Drake's brother John was the first to see her, and three hours later the *Golden Hind* ranged alongside. The Spaniard yielded without resistance: indeed, she could do nothing else, for the captain and crew had 'not even a rapier to defend themselves with'. A contemporary Portuguese account says that the value of her cargo taken by Drake amounted to nearly one and a quarter million Spanish ducats in silver and gold, in addition to pearls and other gems of inestimable worth. The company of the *Golden Hind* long enjoyed the joke of the pilot's boy on the captured vessel: 'Our ship,' he remarked, 'should no longer be called *Spitfire*, but *Spit-Silver*. Yours is the *Spitfire*.' Throughout the treasure-raid, no blood was unnecessarily shed, and no prisoners carried away. Drake wanted the Spaniards' gold, but he was a merciful man and did not want their lives.

Golden Hind now had as much treasure in her hold as she could carry, and there was no object in remaining longer on the coast. The Spaniards, expecting that she would return to the Atlantic through the Straits of Magellan, sent ships south in the hope of catching her. Drake, however, had other ideas – whether or not they formed a part of his original plan. What he did was to work northward as far as about 45° North latitude, and, after refitting *Golden Hind* and scrubbing her clean, to lay a course westward across the Pacific and so return home after circumnavigating the globe. One reason for this decision was to avoid the trap which he knew was laid for him at the Magellan Straits; but there was also a more positive object – to open a trade with the spice islands of the East Indies.

On 13 October 1579, land was sighted, after some twelve weeks at sea, and a month later Drake was in the Moluccas. At the island of Ternate he concluded some sort of agreement with the reigning sultan, who was hostile to the Portuguese there, for a trade monopoly, and took aboard a few tons of spices. Then course was laid for the Cape of Good Hope and home.

Somewhere south of Celebes the voyage nearly ended in disaster. In that difficult and dangerous region of the sea, much cumbered with reefs and islands, which Drake was traversing for the first time and without charts or sailing directions, *Golden Hind* ran hard on a sunken rock. She remained fast for twenty hours and nothing they could do would get her off. Then – 'as it were in a moment by the special grace of God' – the wind shifted, they got sail on her again, and she blew clear. By a miracle no damage had been done. For another month the *Golden Hind* was picking her way amongst reefs and shoals, in constant danger, until she brought up in Java. Thence she ran direct to the Cape of Good Hope, which she passed close aboard – 'a most stately thing and the fairest cape we saw in the whole circumference of the earth' – and, after a call at Sierra Leone, came to her anchor in Plymouth Sound on 3 November 1580.

To wonder at the great consequences which follow upon small accidents has always amused speculative minds: it may well be that but for that shift of wind in the eastern archipelago on 9 January 1579, the subsequent history of Europe might have followed a very different course. If Drake had failed to come home, it is not unlikely that the cautious policy of Burghley might have prevailed, until the growing strength of Spain had become supreme. Even as it was, Elizabeth hesitated, and it was only after six months had passed that she openly declared herself. *Golden Hind* was brought to Deptford, and on her deck Drake received the accolade. It was a momentous occasion. Sir Francis Drake was proclaimed to the world as the man who had struck a blow at Spain, not as a private adventurer, but as the acknowledged servant of the Queen. Soon he would strike many more.

After 1581 events moved quickly towards war. King Philip had invaded Portugal and thus greatly increased his power by control of the Portuguese possessions in Africa and the East Indies. In 1584 William of Orange had been murdered by an agent of Spain; the Spanish ambassador in England had been implicated in an attempted assassination of Elizabeth; in the following year English merchant ships in Spanish ports were seized. It was no time for the Queen to disguise any longer the fact that the greatest weapon which England possessed – her growing power at sea – was to be used openly in England's service. Short of an open declaration of war, she was prepared for anything. Drake, therefore, was commissioned to lead a fresh expedition to attack the Spanish possessions in the West Indies, and thus attempt to cripple, or at least postpone, the Spanish design, now believed to be imminent, of an invasion of England.

The fleet was much larger than any he had yet commanded; it consisted of twenty-nine ships, two of them belonging to the Queen's navy, the rest, after the fashion of that age in which public funds were small, belonging to private owners who risked their property in the simultaneous service of their country and their own pockets. As it turned out, the investors lost money, but Drake added to his reputation, and further proof was given of what could be done by a nation which was supreme at sea. The object of the expedition, besides the usual one of fluttering the Spanish dovecotes in the West Indian islands and on the Main, was to capture and hold some seaport from which it would be possible to cut the Spanish treasure route permanently. It is evident from a contemporary account – the writer of which mentions it casually as if it were something everyone was aware of – that the place Drake was after was Panama. Indeed, he had never given up the idea of holding Panama, knowing, quite rightly, that the loss of it would be a desperate blow to Spain. Once again, however, he was to fail in this great design, this time by ill-luck.

The fleet sailed in September 1585, with Frobisher as vice-admiral and Christopher Carleil, a fine soldier, in command of the land forces. Drake went first to the Spanish coast, cheerfully entered the port of Vigo, where he watered his ships and completed his fitting-out, and then sailed for the Canaries and the Cape Verde islands. He approached Palma in the Canaries, but did not go ashore because of the 'vile sea-gate and the naughtiness' of the only landing place; in the Cape Verde islands, he captured two towns, but lost more than he gained, for it was here that fever took hold of his ships' companies and caused very serious mortality. Arrived in the Caribbean, he stopped a week or two at an uninhabited island to let his sick men get ashore for a while and to clean up the pestilence-ridden ships, and then went straight for San Domingo, the capital city of the island of Hispaniola. With his usual surprise tactics he took the town without difficulty, destroyed or carried off its guns, and demanded a ransom before he would leave. An incident took place here which has been variously interpreted: having occasion to discuss matters with the Spanish commander, Drake sent a Negro boy to him with a flag of truce. The boy was met on his way by some Spanish officers, one of whom 'struck him through the body with his horseman's staff'. He struggled back to where Drake was waiting, and was just able to tell him what happened before he died. 'Greatly passioned' by this (says the old account) Drake promptly hanged two Spanish friars out of a number which were in his hands, and threatened to hang two more every day until the boy's murderer was given up to justice. The culprit was executed by his own people in sight of the English army. What was it that enraged Drake? Was it the violation of the accepted laws of war? or the brutal killing of a young Negro? One would like to think it was the latter; but to do so might well be a mis-reading of the spirit of the times. Not the least of Drake's claims to honour was his avoidance of unnecessary bloodshed and humane treatment of prisoners, and it is tempting to set the general attitude of the English adventurers towards the native inhabitants of the New World against the barbarities, so eloquently chronicled by Raleigh, of their Spanish masters; it is doubtless right to contrast the behaviour of the English with such horrible incidents as that of the Spanish slave-owner who, when his slaves threatened mass suicide, told them that he would kill himself in their company, so that he could continue to torment them in the world beyond the grave. The English are, and perhaps always were, the least bloodthirsty of civilized nations; yet one must remember that Drake's Negro boy, for whom the friars were hanged, had himself been kidnapped out of his African home by English slave-merchants, and that the brave Cimaroons, with whom Drake and Oxenham worked in friendly cooperation, were the kinsmen of slaves sold to the Spanish colonists out of English ships. Drake, like all other Englishmen of his time, saw no evil in slaving, and two hundred years were yet to pass before the dawn even in English minds of the idea that human life might in itself be a sacred thing. Circumstance can bring back the night again, even today.

From Hispaniola Drake sailed for Cartagena on the mainland coast. He had been to Cartagena before and knew the place well. The town was built on an isthmus and strongly fortified, but once again surprise and daring got the English in. It was Carleil's battle; he led his men by night along the edge of the sea, and at low tide forced his way round the barricade where it stopped short at the water, and after a brief struggle was master of the town. As at San Domingo, guns and defences were destroyed, and ransom demanded. Drake was six weeks at Cartagena. The fever was still raging amongst his men and the mortality was still dangerously high. Before he sailed, it was decided at a conference of his captains that the force was too much weakened to undertake the capture of Nombre de Dios and the overland march to Panama. He had to be content with what had been done – considerable damage to Spanish property, much more to Spanish prestige, and the demonstration to the world of how much depended upon the bold and imaginative use of sea-power.

The Queen, though she loved her seamen, never fully learned the lesson they tried so hard to teach her. If Drake, after his return from the Indies in 1586, had been sent back with a fresh and larger force, he might well have succeeded in permanently cutting the Spanish treasure route by the occupation of Panama. But this was not done, and King Philip's preparations for the invasion of England went on with all possible speed. The date fixed for the attempt was the autumn of 1587. The danger was growing, and the services of Drake, now universally recognized as England's greatest sea-captain, were again required. This time he was to attack Spain not indirectly by way of her colonies, but directly in her own ports, where her invasion fleet was building and fitting out for the coming enterprise. With twenty-three ships and some 2,000 men Drake sailed in the spring of 1587 straight for Cadiz. Without hesitation and against the advice of William Borough, his second-in-command, he entered the harbour, followed by the whole fleet. It was packed with shipping and strongly defended by batteries ashore and a fleet of oared galleys, supposed to be more than a match for sailing ships in narrow waters. Drake soon showed that the English gunnery was equal to them. He sank or burned over thirty Spanish ships, including a fine galleon of 1,200 tons belonging to the Marquis of Santa Cruz, the high-admiral of Spain – a loss which 'bred such a corrosive in his heart', as the old writer put it, that the unhappy marquis 'never enjoyed good day after, but within a few months

35

died of extreme grief'. The English fleet got away without the loss of a ship.

After a land action at Sagres, Drake went north again to Lisbon, hoping to engage the fleet of Santa Cruz. He anchored outside and sent word to the marquis that he was 'ready to exchange certain bullets with him'; but the challenge was refused. Then he sailed for the Azores, and some sixty miles off St Michael's sighted a Portuguese carrack homeward bound from the East Indies with a cargo of spices. She was the *San Philip*, and the first East Indiaman to fall into English hands; her cargo was the richest single prize that Drake had ever taken.

Odd though it seems, England was still not officially at war with Spain, and the Queen, when Drake returned, did her best to play down his exploits on the Spanish coast. Drake and Hawkins, the two men who saw most clearly how the newly forged weapon of naval supremacy might be used, must have chafed bitterly at her indecision. The action at Cadiz, and the months of raiding amongst the small shipping on the coast, had weakened the invasion fleet which Philip was preparing, but by no means crippled it. The work went relentlessly on, though the date of the enterprise was now postponed to the following year. It was not till the spring of 1588 that the Queen abandoned all hope of peace.

Communications in those days were slow, and the actual appearance of the Armada off the Lizard in July took the English navy by surprise. Three-quarters of the English force were refitting in Plymouth after an abortive attempt to engage the enemy on the Spanish coast; the remainder were cruising at the eastern end of the Channel to assist the blockade of the Netherlands ports, from which the Spanish army under Parma was known to be awaiting a chance to invade. The weather was fine, the wind southerly or south-westerly; had the Spaniards chosen to enter Plymouth Sound, they would have caught the English ships where they had no room to manoeuvre, and might have done irreparable damage. But the great fleet of 160 sail passed on to the eastward. The English were under the command of Lord Charles Howard of Effingham, with Drake as his second-in-command, supported by John Hawkins and Sir Martin Frobisher, two seamen only less distinguished than himself. The story goes – and one likes to believe that it is true – that Drake and his fellow-captains were playing bowls on the Hoe when the Spanish fleet was sighted; and Lord Howard, on calling for an immediate conference, was calmly answered by Drake that there was 'time to finish the game and to beat the Spaniards too'. The spirit of the tale, with its English gaiety and light-hearted courage, is genuine enough; but one must be very sure that, bowls or no bowls, the fleet lost as little time as possible in getting to sea. With the wind coming into the Sound it was no easy task, but by dawn the following morning the ships were clear of the land, and making for the westward in order to have the Spaniards under their lee. The long running fight had begun. In the light weather of that July it took the Armada a week to run from the Lizard to the Straits of Dover; the purpose of Medina Sidonia was to break the blockade of the Flemish ports and enable the Spanish troops in the Netherlands to be ferried across to the English east coast, but the English commanders were never certain that an attempt would not be made to seize some port on the Channel and effect a landing there, in spite of the fact that the Armada was off Falmouth at the moment it was first sighted and had not offered to enter that spacious and easy harbour. Nevertheless the anxiety remained until the Spaniards were south of the Isle of Wight, and so to leeward of any suitable harbour. The fighting was spasmodic and indecisive, the English coming in singly or in groups to deliver their broadsides, the Spaniards doing all they could to maintain their cumbrous and massive crescent formation – that 'mortal moon', as it appeared to contemporaries. One night, when the fleets were somewhere between Portland and Torbay, Drake did an odd thing: under orders from the Lord High Admiral he was leading the English squadron, showing a stern-light to enable the others to keep their position. Suddenly he extinguished his light and disappeared. Apparently he thought he had seen some of the Spanish ships coming back on their tracks to windward and making for Torbay. But he was mistaken. He left the squadron to fend for themselves. No good had been done – except to himself; for a Spanish ship, already disabled, fell to him as a prize. By modern ideas of discipline such an action would be unpardonable; and even by Elizabethan standards there is not much to be said for it; but it was all in Drake's character. He was never a good subordinate.

The end of the fight is too well known to need retelling. The Spaniards anchored off Calais; Drake's fireships drove them from their anchorage in confusion. The battle of Gravelines followed, and the Armada, still a great fleet though badly mauled, made its way in worsening weather northward up the coast, in the hope of returning to Spain by way of the Orkneys and the Pentland Firth. The English followed, though all their powder was spent, and it was left to the weather to complete the invaders' ruin. Half of the Spanish fleet was wrecked during the course of its perilous voyage, and the menace of invasion was, for the moment, gone –

> The mortal moon has her eclipse endured
> And the sad augurs mock their own presage;
> Incertainties now crown themselves assured
> And peace proclaims olives of endless age.

So, at least, it appeared to Shakespeare in that time of

national rejoicing. Unhappily, however, the olives of peace are as mortal as all other things. On this occasion they never even came into leaf, and the war dragged on.

The following year, 1589, Drake was employed on a new expedition, to restore Don Antonio to the throne of Portugal. It was a failure, and for four years after his return to Plymouth Drake did not go to sea. He lived in his house, Buckland Abbey, sat in Parliament, and interested himself in local affairs at Plymouth. The days of his glory were over, but, like nearly all the other great sea-captains of that time – like Hawkins, Frobisher, Gilbert, Raleigh – he was to give his life for his country. The story of his last service is a melancholy one, as the story of genius in decline cannot fail to be. Drake had worked himself out, and after the year of the Armada he never recovered the brilliant dash, the power of swift decision, the gay recklessness of his challenge to fate, which in the old days had made him supreme amongst the seamen of the world. Apart from sheer ability and native courage Drake's distinctive qualities were the qualities proper to youth, and he, like all men, when his time came, could not choose but be old.

In 1595 the Queen decided to make one more attempt to cut the Spanish treasure-route from the New World, and a fleet was equipped to sail under the joint command of Drake and Hawkins. It was not a happy combination, and the whole enterprise was undermined by dissension from the start. At the very beginning of the voyage, one ship of the fleet grounded on the Eddystone: it was an ill omen. Drake wished, as he had always wished, to go once more for Panama; but Spanish raids on the Cornish coast had made the Queen fear that a fresh attempt at invasion might be imminent, and she forbade the two admirals to be absent for longer than six months. Then news came that a great treasure galleon had been forced by weather into Puerto Rico, the most easterly of the large islands in the Caribbean. Thither the fleet sailed, but not in time to prevent the Spaniards from getting wind of its purpose and sending a warning to the garrison. Hawkins died before the fleet arrived; Drake, now in sole command, anchored off the harbour. His attempt to capture the town did not succeed. Then he sailed for Nombre de Dios, ignoring the Queen's instructions to be home in six months. The familiar little port was taken, and Sir Thomas Baskerville, in command of the land forces, was sent ashore to lead his men to Panama. But things were different on the isthmus from what they had been twenty-three years before: the Spaniards were in much greater strength; they were on the alert, and the Cima-roons had been brought under control. Baskerville was ambushed and forced to retreat. He rejoined Drake at Nombre de Dios with nothing accomplished. Again – and now for the last time – Drake had failed to capture Panama. Early in the following winter the fleet sailed, and at Porto Bello some ten miles west of Nombre de Dios, on 28 January 1596, Drake died of an attack of dysentery. He had been ill for a fortnight. Just before he died, he struggled from his bed, dressed himself, and spoke to the ship's company. Perhaps he tried to cheer them, but his heart must have been bitter. Sir Thomas Baskerville brought the fleet home to England. It was a sorrowful home-coming to Plymouth, which never again would see the two greatest of her sons.

Drake had his private enemies, but from the time of his triumphant entry into Plymouth Sound on that Sunday in the year 1573 with his little vessel ballasted with Spanish gold, he was a national hero, as he has ever since remained. Like Shakespeare himself, in that burning and brilliant age, Drake was but one amongst many of his kind, though the greatest. It was the age when modern England finally took shape both in her own consciousness and in the eyes of the world, at last turning away from continental entanglements and seeking her true source of greatness and power in world-wide commerce, colonization, and oceanic enterprise. For the men of the first Elizabethan age, sea-power ceased to be merely the means of defence against invasion; it became the means of limitless expansion and pointed the way to the crippling of the mighty military empire of Spain. How it could be used was demonstrated over and over again by a dozen of reckless and gallant captains, but by none so brilliantly as by Drake in the great years before the Armada. To Drake more than to any man (except perhaps to Hawkins, whose magnificent work as controller of the navy must never be forgotten) were due the tactical developments which revolutionized war at sea: the design of the new ships, built low and longer, for speed and power of manoeuvre, and the broadside fired through gun-ports in the ship's side. In the Spanish ships of Drake's day, the fighting men were still the soldiers, who waited for a chance to grapple and board; but Drake's ships were units of offence; they were mobile batteries, and all aboard them were seamen – men and officers, both those who worked the ship and those who served the guns. Drake's order at Port St Julian that the gentleman should haul with the mariner was a momentous one in the history of the British Navy. He was a fitting memorial not only in the impressive statue which stands on Plymouth Hoe and looks out over Drake's Island and Drake's Passage in the Sound below, but in the Sound itself, still one of the finest of English harbours, and still used for purposes of peace and war which Drake would appreciate as well as any man, and better than most.

Dr Johnson

SOMEBODY once remarked at a party, at which Dr Johnson was present, that the life of a mere literary man could not be very entertaining. 'But it certainly may,' Johnson replied. 'Why should the life of a literary man be less entertaining than the life of any other man? Are there not interesting varieties in such a life? As a *literary life* it may be very entertaining.'

Johnson was right, as he usually was. A literary life may be very entertaining indeed – which is not surprising when one considers that the arts are the crowning achievement of civilized man, and that of all the arts literature is the noblest. One must be very dull indeed to find lack of entertainment in the lives of men of letters. Nevertheless, just how entertaining those lives can be, even Johnson himself never knew, for the obvious reason that he did not read the biography of himself by his brilliant and devoted friend Boswell – a book which, to adapt a phrase from one of its many editors, contains as much of the 'marrow and fatness' of human life and experience as any book ever written. If Boswell had never written his biography – his two biographies, rather; for his *Journal of a Tour to the Hebrides* is only less valuable and amusing than his *Life of Johnson* – we should know Johnson as a powerful and dominant figure in eighteenth-century literature, the author of three major contributions to literary history and scholarship, a critic of narrow range but superb vigour and acumen, an essayist with a profound knowledge of the darker side of human experience, enlivened, nevertheless, with a continuous undercurrent of wit and flashes of unexpected gaiety, and master of a style which, at its worst, is somewhat over-formal and elaborate, and, at its best – contrary to the belief of those who have never read him – as sharp and supple as a rapier. We should know him, that is, as one amongst the dozen or so of the great prose writers of England. But Boswell did write his two biographical books, and the result is that we know Johnson as something more than a very distinguished writer: we know him also as a man with a combination of qualities, to which only malignity could deny the title of greatness; for under his intellectual self-confidence was a profound moral humility; his intense enjoyment of the good things of life – good food, good friends, good books – was, as it were, the surface-glitter on an unplumbed sea of physical pain and mysterious spiritual terrors; and behind his arrogant and often brutal manner was an almost divine tenderness of heart. Above all, we know him as a great Englishman; for Johnson was English to the core and marrow of his being. He was English in his oddities and contradictions, English in his insularity and prejudice, English in the superb common sense which would not allow the reasoning of a subtle intellect to prevail over the test of direct experience, English in his admiration of rank and order combined with a love of men, simply as men and without respect to either, despising no human weaknesses, except cruelty, pretentiousness, and impiety – and English, too, in his love of a lark, as when, at the age of fifty, he tried to persuade an eminent and learned friend to join him in climbing over a wall in Oxford, or when, six years earlier, he was knocked up by two young friends at three in the morning. 'What, is it you, you dogs?' he cried. 'I'll have a frisk with you.' So off they went to Covent Garden market, whence, finding their attempts to help the fruiterers arrange their hampers were not required, they repaired to a tavern and drank bishop until breakfast time. Finally, he was English in the uncompromising sanity of his attitude to literature, his own domain in which he was king: 'The only end of writing', he said, 'is to enable the readers better to enjoy life, or better to endure it.' There are writers and critics today who might with advantage take that to heart.

One aspect of greatness is the power some men have had not only to achieve notable things but to draw into themselves, as into a focal point, the larger and more scattered elements of thought, or feeling, or motive, which are characteristic of their time, so that such men come in a unique way to express their epoch for us, to represent it humanly and intelligibly, much as a portrait painter draws together into his picture of a face the diffused elements of character of which he is aware in the person to whom the face belongs. Thus the active and adventurous side of the Elizabethan age is focused for us in Drake, its imaginative and poetic side in Shakespeare, so that Drake is not a great seaman only, or Shakespeare a great poet only, but each in his own way is also a mirror of England, or of an epoch of English history, to a degree not attained by other seamen or other poets of the period. Thus Johnson, too, brings to a focus for us the scattered rays of a period of social history; in him more than in any other man we can see the image of literary London in the eighteenth century. And if anyone should say that he does not wish to see the image of literary London in the eighteenth century, there is no need for him to fret; for he will see Johnson himself first. Human nature has a mystery similar to the mystery of art: for as a work of art becomes universal only by virtue of its particularity, so it is only by being most himself that a man can become *representative*. There was nobody like Johnson, and never will be. He had drawn into himself the invisible influences of his time, and transmuted them into something inimitable and unique. That he was an odd man, the following pages will show – but England is the land of eccentrics, and we like a man none the less for being odd. We admire reason and talk much in its praise, but our sense of life is too strong to allow us to live by it – which is why many foreigners call us mad. Johnson was an eccentric, for all his magnificent reasonableness, and his eccentricity endears him to us, as it endeared him to his friends. He had many friends, and of the multitude who were acquainted with him, all respected him, though some were envious, and a few were scared. Mrs Boswell, indeed, did not like him much: perhaps she too was jealous – or perhaps she merely deprecated too much candle-grease on her drawing-room carpet. But even Mrs Boswell respected him; she could hardly fail to do so, knowing, as everyone else knew, that in Johnson, more than in any man living, were the three radical virtues of honesty, kindness, and courage, from which all other virtues spring. So we may pardon her for pettishly remarking, when she found her husband deeply absorbed in his strange new friend, that, though she had heard of a man leading a bear, she had never yet known of a bear leading a man.

Samuel Johnson was born at Lichfield, in Staffordshire, on 18 September 1709 – a large and ugly baby. His father, Michael Johnson, was a bookseller and stationer in that city, a man of strong native sense and some learning, but no fortune. Once a week he kept an open bookstall in the streets of Birmingham; he died even poorer than he had lived. Mrs Johnson had no interest in books; she was a kindly woman and a good mother; her son loved and honoured her, and was her main support during the long years of her widowhood, until she died at the age of ninety, when Johnson himself was fifty. One of his best-known books, *Rasselas*, he wrote in the evenings of a single week, to pay the expenses of her funeral.

There is no need to repeat the anecdotes, some of them

apocryphal, of Johnson's precocity. It is not, after all, to be expected that a man of brilliant parts should have been a stupid child. Naturally, he took early to books, especially romances, which he continued to enjoy throughout his life. It is more important at the moment to remember the body he was born with, than the mind. He was excessively near-sighted, one eye being almost blind – 'the dog', as he once put it, 'was never good for much'. Coming home from school as a child, he would go down on hands and knees to get a sight of the kerb before he ventured to cross the road. Once in his later years, in the garden of a country house, his host, hoping to lead the talk to scientific subjects, asked his guest if he was a botanist. 'No, sir,' Johnson replied; 'I am not a botanist; and should I wish to become a botanist, I must first turn myself into a *reptile*.' He had the scrofula, or King's Evil (and was 'touched' for it by Queen Anne at the age of three), a glandular complaint which manifests itself by pits and scars on the flesh of face and neck. He suffered from a convulsive tic. He muttered to himself. His movements were spasmodic and uncontrolled: to the end of his life he walked like one struggling in chains; when he rode, he could not control his horse, but was carried along, as Boswell tells us, 'as if in a balloon'. His frame was big-boned, and powerful in spite of its defects: attacked in the street by four ruffians at once, he tackled the lot and kept them at bay until the watch arrived, and put them (and him) in the roundhouse; having his chair at the theatre taken by a stranger, who refused a polite request to give it up, Johnson tossed him, chair and all, into the pit. He was a strong and fearless swimmer. At the age of sixty-six he challenged his friend Baretti to a race in the rain in the streets of Paris, and beat him. Disease had a hard task to get the better of his tough and muscular body, and of his almost invincible vitality. Added to his physical disabilities, perhaps in part consequent upon them, was a constitutional black melancholy, which made him dread solitude and gave a permanently gloomy tone to his thoughts. Indolent by nature, he worked – and no man worked harder – by an effort of will, and at extraordinary pressure and speed. He wrote forty-eight pages of his *Life of Savage* in the course of a night, and one of his weekly essays for the *Rambler* in half an hour. He was often morose and irritable. He had strong passions and appetites, which he could subdue, but never moderate. These qualities – the scarred flesh, the blind eye, the ungainly body; the weight of despondency and indolence, the fierce desires, the vision, too early seen, of the harshness and dark menace of life in this world – were not an augury of ease to the son of a poor provincial bookseller. He went to school, learned his lessons not without the stick – for which he was afterwards grateful – and, at the age of eighteen, upon the promise (which was not fulfilled) of a friend to pay his expenses, was entered a commoner of Pembroke College in Oxford. As the coach was about to leave Lichfield to take Johnson to Oxford for the first time, old Dame Oliver, who had taught him his letters as a child, brought him a present of gingerbread and said he was the best scholar she had ever had. Unlike others who have risen from obscurity to eminence, he always remembered this with pleasure.

He remained at Oxford just over a year, reading desultorily, and too poor to buy new shoes. He had a reputation for wildness, but said himself in later years that his neglect of decorum was only a mask for misery, due to his poverty and the melancholia which now seized him with such force that he feared for his sanity. Then his father died, insolvent, and the brief career at the university was over. Johnson returned to Lichfield without a degree, and began to look about for a way of supporting himself.

He had already much learning, acquired in his own odd way. He never read a book through. 'What?' was his habitual question to anyone who chanced to speak in praise of a book, 'What? Did you read it through?' But he had the faculty of seizing at once upon whatever was valuable in a book – and of never forgetting it. With a mind well stored, but penniless and obscure, he found (as many have found since) but one profession open to him – teaching in school. The school which offered him a post was in the small town of Market Bosworth, and there Johnson worked for a year and a half. He was bored and miserable. For a while he earned a few small sums with his pen; then, when he was twenty-five, he married. His wife was a Mrs Porter, a widow whom he had met three years before. She was forty-seven, and not beautiful. Johnson himself was now a gaunt young man, lank, and of great stature, his face seamed and scarred, his straight, stiff hair parted behind, his voice loud and commanding – a forbidding figure. It was the strangest marriage, but a true one. For sixteen years Johnson gave his 'Tetty' his faithful and devoted love, and for the rest of his long life kept the anniversary of her death, with Easter and Good Friday, as a day of fasting and prayer. After she died he preserved her wedding ring in a little, round wooden box, inside the lid of which he had pasted a slip of paper with the dates of their marriage and her death:

> The ring, so worn as you behold,
> So thin, so pale, is yet of gold:
> The passion such it was to prove –
> Worn with life's care, love yet was love.

The lines are George Crabbe's – but they might have been Johnson's. Many people, some of Johnson's friends amongst them, have laughed at his marriage; but it is always easy, and nearly always foolish, to laugh at other men's loves.

After his marriage, he opened a school of his own, at Edial, near Lichfield. That, at least, was his intention; but though he rented a large house and advertised its purpose in the *Gentleman's Magazine*, he got three pupils only. One of them was David Garrick, destined to be Johnson's lifelong friend and to win fame as the greatest actor of the age. He would have been surprised indeed, as a small boy in that academy, had he known that his instructor, often passionate and always bored, with his queer mannerisms and queerer wife, was one day to write about him that sentence of splendid praise, describing how his death 'eclipsed the gaiety of nations and impoverished the world's stock of harmless pleasure'. The new school soon came to an end, and Johnson, in company with Garrick and with $2\frac{1}{2}d$. in his pocket, set off in the coach for London. His real life was about to begin.

Thenceforward London was Johnson's spiritual home. He identified himself with London, and loved it. He loved the sense of packed humanity, the bustle and infinite variety of business, the concentration there of England's brightest intellectual life: it was his best defence against solitude and the dark thoughts which were never far beneath the surface of his mind. 'When a man', he said, 'is tired of London he is tired of life.' He had no use for country pleasures; the best he could say of the Brighton downs was that they were so desolate that 'if one *had* a mind to hang oneself, no tree could be found on which to tie the rope'. People were what Johnson loved, not 'dead nature', as Charles Lamb once naughtily called it in a letter to Wordsworth. For him, the full tide of life was to be found at Charing Cross. 'Is not this very fine?' he once remarked to Boswell, when they were spending the day in Greenwich Park. 'Yes, sir,' said Boswell, 'but not so fine as Fleet Street.' 'You are right sir,' Johnson replied. He loved London's violent, vigorous, and teeming life, the contrast of its squalor and splendour, the houses of the great and the little packed courts and alleys of the poor; the mere size of the great city delighted him, and the number and variety and strangeness of the things men did to earn their bread. Once he surprised his friends by telling them why the London poor collected bones from the gutters, and what use they put them to – and advised them, on another occasion, to explore Wapping. No phase of life was too mean to interest him; to be human was enough to awaken his regard, as to be miserable was, in Goldsmith's words, enough to ensure his protection.

Johnson's early years in London he spent without his wife, whom he left in Lichfield and visited when he could. He never told anyone very much about those years; he gave hints only, in conversation, and here and there in his writings. It was a time of the bitterest poverty. He made friends with Richard Savage, a man of extraordinary character who may, or may not, have been an impostor; and he has described in his *Life* how many occasions, when he was without a penny, Savage would walk the streets till he was weary and lie down 'in the summer upon a bulk, or in the winter, with his associates in poverty, among the ashes of a glass-house'. Probably there were nights when Johnson shared those beds. There were certainly days when he was hungry; and his clothes were so shabby that he shrank from appearing before people who knew him: an acquaintance has related how once, in a chop-house, his dinner was sent to him behind a screen. His present poverty was harder to bear than his poverty at Oxford; then, he thought he had someone to support him; now he knew that he had no one. He was writing hard, trying to scrape what he could to get him a dinner – 'I dined very well', he used to say, 'for eightpence, with very good company, at the Pine Apple in New Street. I had a cut of meat for sixpence, and bread for a penny, and gave the waiter a penny; so that I was quite well served, nay, better than the rest, for they gave the waiter nothing.' The writing was hack-work for the booksellers, with an occasional paper in the *Gentleman's Magazine*, for which he also 'did' the parliamentary debates. He was unknown, and the work wretchedly paid. The black melancholy was still on him, a vile, ineradicable weed in a spirit hungry for life.

When he was twenty-nine he published anonymously a poem: *London*. Pope, whose word upon poetry was law, noticed it, praised it, and asked the name of the author. On being told that he was some obscure person called Johnson, Pope said, 'He will soon be *déterré*'. It was Johnson's first success: he sold the poem for £10. It was a good enough poem of its type and period, though few would read it today except out of love for its author. Observation of men and manners, the power of generalizing from the particular, sound sentiments, good morality; and the whole expressed, to render it pleasing and memorable, in precise and pointed verse: such a description fits not too badly a great deal of the poetry of Johnson's age. 'I can make verses easily enough,' he once said, 'but the difficulty is to know when I have made good ones.' The remark is full of suggestion of what poetry meant for him, and for many, perhaps most, of his contemporaries. It was not then an autonomous art, as it had previously been, as it was to become in the succeeding age, and as it has remained ever since; it was but one accomplishment of a civilized and cultivated person. The notion, to us a commonplace, that poetry is a unique world, with its own laws and its own enchantment, would have made Johnson and his contemporaries stare.

For a professional writer in eighteenth-century London there was more labour and less reward than there is today. Johnson had no wish to live by his pen. He took little pleasure in the drudgery of composition. 'No man', he said in his blunt and uncompromising way, 'ever wrote except to get money.' But money had to be got somehow; for a time, after the publication of *London*, he had thoughts of becoming a lawyer, and even, on the recommendation of friends, of taking the mastership of another school. But he had no university degree, and neither of these schemes proved practicable. So it was write or starve. He wrote hard and industriously, by little and little making his way, and at the same time – which was even more important to him – making friends. It may seem odd that a writer of Johnson's calibre should have found nothing but drudgery in the exercise of his craft. Indeed, it seemed odd to Boswell. 'I wonder, sir,' he once remarked to Johnson, when, in the years of his greater prosperity, he had let time go by with nothing done, 'that you have not more pleasure in writing, than in not writing.' 'Sir,' Johnson replied, 'you *may* wonder.' Literature he loved; he was said to know more books than any man alive; but he had little desire to write them. He preferred to talk.

His first great contribution to English letters was begun in 1747, when he was thirty-eight, though he had no doubt been turning it over in his mind for several years before that. This was his *English Dictionary*. It was a tremendous task for one man to undertake, as Johnson was well aware; he hoped to accomplish it in three years, and when his friend Dr Adams reminded him that the forty members of the French Academy had spent forty years in compiling their dictionary, 'Let me see,' Johnson replied, 'forty times forty is sixteen hundred. As three to sixteen hundred, so is the proportion of an Englishman to a Frenchman.' In point of fact, the work took eight years to complete – and it won him international fame. After the publication of the Dictionary, Johnson was universally recognized as the foremost man of letters of the age; the University of Oxford made him a Master of Arts, the

University of Dublin a Doctor of Laws. One of his greatest griefs was that his wife did not live to share his triumph. The Dictionary was a noble achievement of scholarship and learning, and though its usefulness today is overlaid by the immense advance in the science of lexicography since Johnson's day, we should remember that Johnson himself, the least conceited of men, would be the first to rejoice in that advance if he were here to see it. Few dictionaries are happy hunting-grounds for jokes; but Johnson's contains several – small ironies slipped in to lighten his labour, as when he defines *Lexicographer* as 'a maker of dictionaries: *a harmless drudge*', or adds to his definition of *oats* the irrelevant but pleasing fact that it is 'the food of horses in England, and of men in Scotland'. Johnson also made mistakes – how should he not? He admitted them readily: asked by a lady how he came to define *pastern* as 'the knee of a horse', 'Ignorance, madam, pure ignorance,' was his unruffled answer. He made little money by the Dictionary; the price paid by the booksellers (the system of royalties had not been introduced in Johnson's day) was £1,575, but most of this sum was used to meet the necessary expenses involved, the chief of which was the employment of six amanuenses. He was occupied with much other work at the same time, most notably his *Rambler*, a weekly essay on life and manners. The eight years spent on the Dictionary were the busiest and most productive of his literary life; the last two of them, after his wife's death, were also the most darkened and oppressed by the mysterious shadow which only the actual presence of a friend could ever, even momentarily, dissipate. This dreadful affliction must never be left out of account in appreciating Johnson's character or in estimating his achievement. The most sociable of men, he courted society not only for the delight he took in it, but to escape from the terrors of solitude: often, he tells us, he would escort his guests at their departure to the foot of the stairs, in the hope that they might turn back, and prolong the talk of which he had dreaded the ending. He could play the fool like a boy, when the mood was on him, and laugh with Fanny Burney or Hester Thrale as gaily as any man; but his settled conviction was that life was a thing to be endured rather than enjoyed. Few men have accomplished a greater body of work; yet by nature he was indolent and dilatory. Magnificently sane, he was pursued throughout his life by the fear of madness; and good beyond most men's measure, he was haunted by the fear of hell. What is the explanation of the fact that the eighteenth century, the Age of Reason, was darkened, so far as the writers then living were concerned, by the menace of insanity more than any other? Smart and Collins went mad; Cowper was on the verge of madness; Johnson dreaded it – and only a little later there were the Lambs, and their friend Charles Lloyd, and poor John Clare. Johnson told nobody, except, possibly, Mrs Thrale, of his secret misery; it is revealed to us in a little journal which was not destroyed when, just before his death, he burnt most of his private papers.

In 1762, two years after the accession of George III, Johnson was granted a pension of £300 a year by the King, and thus freed for the remainder of his life from the menace of want and the necessity of writing for bread. When the offer was made, he was unwilling to accept it until he knew for certain that he would not be required to use his talents in the interest of the administration. 'Pray, my lord,' he said to Lord Bute, who was then Prime Minister, 'what am I expected to do for this pension?' 'It is not given you', was Bute's answer, 'for anything that you are to do, but for what you have done.' Had the answer been different, Johnson would certainly have refused it; apart from his contemptuous definition of 'pensioner' in his Dictionary, he had already, on the only occasion of his life when he had sought for patronage, given clear enough proof of his proud and independent spirit. The plan of his Dictionary had been addressed to Lord Chesterfield, who indicated his willingness to support the project. The promise, however, such as it was, was not fulfilled, and throughout the eight years which Johnson spent in writing the Dictionary, he got no help from his intended patron. Nor did he deign to solicit it further. Just before it was published, Lord Chesterfield, who liked to be associated with letters and still, in spite of his neglect, hoped that Johnson might dedicate the work to him, tried to win back Johnson's regard by writing two laudatory papers about him in a current periodical. But the noble earl had misjudged his man. 'Is not a Patron, my Lord,' Johnson replied in his famous letter, 'one who looks with unconcern on a man struggling for life in the water, and, when he has reached ground, encumbers him with help? The notice which you have been pleased to take of my labours, had it been early, had been kind; but it has been delayed till I am indifferent, and cannot enjoy it; till I am solitary, and cannot impart it; till I am known, and do not want it. I hope it is not very cynical asperity not to confess obligations where no benefit has been received, or to be unwilling that the public should consider me as owing that to a Patron, which Providence has enabled me to do for myself.' On a later occasion, when Lord Chesterfield's book *Letters to his Son* was mentioned, Johnson pleasantly remarked that it recommended 'the manners of a dancing master' – and the morals of something worse.

Meanwhile he was occupied with his edition of Shakespeare, the second of his great contributions to English scholarship. The Proposals for this work had been issued as long ago as 1757, and it was not to be finished until 1765. It is easy today to deride Johnson's criticism of Shakespeare, for it belongs to a different world from that to which the criticism of the past hundred and fifty years has accustomed us. It is true that Johnson was blind to one aspect of poetry – to us the most essential; he doubtless smiled at Nash's phrase, if he read it (and he surely did, because he read everything), that poetry is 'the honey of all flowers and the very phrase of Angels'; he was insensible to poetry's spell-binding and incantatory power – as he was insensible also to the power of music: nevertheless the Preface to his Shakespeare is, within its own narrow limits, a model of cool criticism, and still valuable to a modern reader who may, perhaps, have drunk more deeply than his head can stand of the intoxicating Coleridgean wine and of other vintages pressed from grapes grown later in the same fertile soil. Johnson's chief praise of Shakespeare was that he knew men and women, and never talked nonsense about them – or gave them nonsense to talk.

With his Dictionary published and his Shakespeare expected, Johnson was now a familiar and respected figure in his beloved London: the Great Cham of literature, as Smollett the novelist described him, not without envy. In 1763 Boswell, his future biographer, met him for the first time. For us, who enjoy the fruits of it, it was a momentous meeting. Boswell was a young Scotsman of twenty-three, the son of a Scottish law-lord, Lord Auchinleck; he had come to London in the hope of getting a commission in the Guards, and so frustrating his father's efforts to make him an advocate. The hope was not fulfilled; but he met Johnson, and everyone else who was eminent in the intellectual and literary life of London; and that was enough – almost – to make him happy. Vain, warm-hearted, sociable to excess; highly intelligent, well-informed, and with a sense of character amounting to genius; Boswell was, with his blessed faculty of admiration and brilliant literary gift, born to be Johnson's biographer. Johnson at once recognized his quality, and repaid his homage with deep affection and touching gratitude. The meeting took place in the house of the bookseller Davies, a mutual friend, where Boswell was having tea. As they were sitting together, Johnson unexpectedly entered the shop. Boswell was much agitated, for he already knew of the great man's prejudice against the Scotch. 'Don't,' he whispered to Davies, who was about to introduce them, 'don't tell where I come from.' But Davies did. 'Mr Johnson,' said Boswell, 'I do indeed come from Scotland, but I cannot help it.' 'That, sir,' was Johnson's reply, 'is what a very great many of your countrymen cannot help.' It was not a promising beginning; but Boswell had a resilient nature, and a few days later ventured to call upon Johnson at his chambers in the Temple. Johnson was dressed in a rusty brown suit; on his head was a little old unpowdered wig, on his feet a pair of unbuckled shoes by way of slippers; his shirt-neck and the knees of his breeches were loose, his black worsted stockings ill drawn-up, and (as he confessed that very afternoon) he had 'no passion' for clean linen. Boswell's quick eye took in these details at a glance; then Johnson began to talk, and his uncouth appearance was at once forgotten. Boswell listened, and when he rose to leave and thanked his host for allowing him to hear him speak, 'Sir,' Johnson replied, 'I am obliged to any man who visits me'. It was no empty or conventional phrase, but meant sincerely. The twenty years' friendship had begun. To the end of Johnson's life, Gough Square, or Bolt Court, or Johnson's Court – wherever the old man was living – was always Boswell's first place of call, and there, or at the Turk's Head or the Mitre (after the Mermaid, most famous of taverns in English literary history: a plaque marks the site of it in the Strand today), the two men, with other friends, perhaps, of the first distinction in the artistic or intellectual life of London – Garrick, Burke, Goldsmith, or others hardly less eminent

– would sit far into the night, and talk. It was good talk, and time did not exist for the talkers. Once when Boswell reminded Johnson that midnight had struck, 'Sir,' replied Johnson, 'what is that to you and me?' Good talk is a lost art nowadays; we are too busy for it, or pretend to be too busy. Johnson, who got through more work than most of us, always had time. He loved 'to fold his legs and have out his talk'. The flavour of his talk, and of his friends' talk, is still sharp on our lips: for it is treasured up for us in Boswell's book. Talking was Johnson's second art; he was at his very best in congenial company, for then, and only then, the black dog of his melancholy was driven away. Splendid as a writer, he was no less splendid as a talker; formidable, indeed, when the mood was on him and he 'talked for victory', and exulted when it was won – 'if his pistol misses fire, he knocks you down', said Goldsmith, 'with the butt-end' – he could be witty, gay, or profound as the theme required, his immense store of knowledge always at command for illustration or comment, his superb clarity of thought enabling him to penetrate instantly to the heart of an argument. He had the talker's two most enviable gifts: he kept his knowledge accessible, like the owner of a vast library who can put his hand at any moment on the book he needs; and he was never at a loss for the apt and incisive word. Foolish people have mocked at Johnson for his magniloquence: even his own friends sometimes did, as when Goldsmith (who always fretted at his own inability to shine in conversation), explaining to the company that the difficulty in writing a fable about, say, little fishes, was to make them talk like little fishes, and seeing Johnson's huge frame shaking with ominous laughter at a notion so absurd, exclaimed: 'Why, Dr Johnson, this is not so easy as you seem to think; for if you were to make little fishes talk they would talk like whales.' Maybe Johnson did talk like a whale now and then; Boswell tells us as much: 'Generally,' he writes, 'when he had concluded a period, by which time he was a good deal exhausted by violence and vociferation, he used to blow out his breath like a whale. This I suppose was a relief to his lungs; and seemed in him to be a contemptuous mode of expression, as if he had made the arguments of his opponents fly like chaff before the wind.' It was a part of his quality, and his friends loved him for it; but he did not always 'talk for victory'; he by no means always used the pistol, either trigger or butt-end. That was only his fun, as Lamb remarked of the metaphysical disquisitions of Coleridge. To be sure, he enjoyed it; the temptation to knock a man down was not always to be resisted, and he was sometimes rude; 'Sir,' he said to a young man who asked his advice (heaven knows why) on whether or not he should marry, 'I would advise no man to marry who is not likely to propagate understanding.' But the essential quality of Johnson's talk is not to be found in the rollicking blow, the grandiloquent phrase, or the rolling, many-syllabled word – though in all these he delighted; it is to be found in the pure pith of practical good sense, always redeemed from the commonplace by his own inimitable style. In spite of his vast reading, Johnson was not a bookish man; he knew life even better than he knew books. What he knew, he knew absolutely, and from direct experience, and knew that he knew it. All whimsy and unprofitable speculation were abhorrent to him; he did not love, as Sir Thomas Browne did, to lose himself in an *O altitudo*, but kept his feet firmly on earth, as a man amongst men. Two or three grand philosophical principles – the fear of God, the necessity of an ordered society, the duty of charity – governed his thinking, and most of his swift apophthegms, his invincible summings-up of an argument, can be traced to them. Johnson's talk did not open vistas or reveal new truth; it exemplified the stored wisdom of civilized men, as literature, before it grew finical and began to feel an itch for novelty, had its finest passages in illumination of the great commonplaces of human experience, love and death, and the transitoriness of earthly things. Burke, said Goldsmith, would 'wind into a subject like a serpent'; but Johnson would leap upon it. 'He has no formal preparation,' wrote Boswell; 'no flourishing with the sword. He is through your body in an instant.' Once Boswell tried to apologize to him for a woman who had been divorced from her husband; he ran through all the common and specious arguments in her defence – her husband's brutality, the death of their love, her youth and beauty, her desire for happiness with her new lover. But Johnson cut him short: 'My dear sir,' he said 'never accustom your mind to mingle virtue and vice. The woman's a —— and there's an end on't.' Granted the premises (and Johnson's premises, in all matters of conduct and of how life should be lived in the world, never varied), the logic and morality of this are as magnificent as the language in which they are expressed is pointed and racy. 'No man is a hypocrite in his pleasures'; 'a man should keep his friendships always in repair'; 'it is the business of a wise man to be happy'; every other page of Boswell will furnish instances of his sayings. His talk was good talk, because it was as quick as the glance of an eye, as supple as fine steel, and always based firmly on the broad principles of truth as he saw it. Boswell once tried to argue with him in defence of two Methodist undergraduates who were turned out of Oxford. 'Was it not hard', he said 'to expel them? For I am told they were good beings.' 'I believe they might be good beings,' was Johnson's immediate answer; 'but they were not fit to be in the University of Oxford. A cow is a very good animal in the field; but we turn her out of a garden.' Men were Johnson's natural companions, and the talk of men his proper element – once he reproved his friend Langton for

cutting their talk short to keep an appointment for breakfast with a set of '*un-idea'd* girls'; but though the talk of
men was what he loved best, he had much pleasure too in
the talk of women – provided that they had penetration
enough to see that he had (as Goldsmith put it) nothing
of the bear but his skin. One evening when he was
amongst the Blue-stockings, Miss Monckton, who was
noted for her wit, remarked that some of Sterne's writings
were very pathetic. Johnson denied it. 'I am sure', said
Miss Monckton, 'they have affected *me*.' 'Why,' replied
Johnson, 'that is because, dearest, you're a dunce.'
Fanny Burney records in her diary that he had more fun
and comical humour and love of nonsense about him
than almost anybody she ever saw. It is an aspect to be
remembered of the man who could say, after a visit to
Ranelagh, that there was not one in all that brilliant
circle who was not *afraid to go home and think*. 'Burton',
wrote Lamb, 'was a man often assailed by deepest
melancholy, and at other times much given to laughing
and jesting, as is the way with melancholy men.' Lamb
assuredly knew this as well as anyone, and he might
have written it with equal justice of Johnson, or of
himself.

From the time that Johnson got his pension, and had
been recognized as the monarch of literary London, the
events of his life can be quickly chronicled. In 1765 his
edition of Shakespeare was published; in the same year
he was introduced to Mr Thrale, the wealthy brewer in
whose family he was to spend many of the happiest days
of his life. Two years later he talked with the King in the
library of the Queen's house in London – for Johnson a
memorable occasion, which he loved to tell of. In the
course of the conversation the King asked him if he was
writing anything at the moment, and Johnson replied
that he was not: he had already, he thought, done his
part as a writer. 'I should have thought so too,' the King

replied, 'if you had not written so well.' Asked, when he was one day recounting this incident, if he had made any reply to this high compliment, 'No, sir,' said Johnson, 'when the King had said it, it was to be so. It was not for me to bandy civilities with my Sovereign.' In 1773 he spent three months with Boswell, touring Scotland and visiting the Hebrides. In 1779–80 the *Lives of the Poets*, his third and last major contribution to literature, was published. In June 1783, he had a paralytic stroke, from which he temporarily recovered. He died without pain on 13 December 1784, and was buried in Westminster Abbey. 'His death', wrote his friend Arthur Murphy, 'kept the public mind in agitation beyond all previous example.'

For a writer to be buried in Westminster Abbey is the highest honour the nation can bestow; and there is no need to question the substantial truth of what Murphy declared to be the effect on the public mind of Johnson's death. Yet England has produced many writers superior to Johnson, great though he was – and not a few of them in his own epoch. One can understand readily enough that the death of Garrick eclipsed the gaiety of nations, for the relationship of an admired and beloved actor with his audience is a peculiarly direct and personal one; it is harder to understand the widespread sense of dereliction at the death of a man of letters. The truth is that in the course of his long life Johnson had come to be valued by his many friends and countless acquaintances even more as a unique and admirable person than as a writer. Perhaps the secret of his hold upon people's minds was the peculiarly happy blend in his character of the dependable and the unexpected, of the eccentricities in expression and behaviour with an underlying and most sovereign sanity of thought. The English, the most imaginative of peoples, as their literature proves, are apt to be ill at ease with the artistic temperament; they will rise with a poem into the intense inane, but are seldom happy to take tea with a poet who habitually dwells there. They are at ease with Johnson, because they recognize in him many of the qualities which they would most like to possess. For Johnson had the very reverse of the artistic temperament: he was, in the best sense, a man of the world. Though his thoughts were often exercised with heaven and hell, he lived amongst men and shared their pleasures, both of the mind and of the body. He took a proper interest in his food: 'Some people', he said, 'have a foolish way of not minding, or pretending not to mind, what they eat. For my part, I mind my belly very studiously; for I look upon it that he who does not mind his belly will hardly mind anything else.' He fancied himself a nice judge of cookery: 'This', he once remarked, 'was a good dinner enough, to be sure; but it was not a dinner to *ask* a man to.' When Mrs Thrale ventured to inquire if he ever used to 'huff' his wife about his meat, 'Yes, yes,' he answered; 'but then she huffed me worse; for she said one day as I was going to say grace: "Nay hold – do not make a farce of thanking God for a dinner which you will presently protest not eatable".' He would put large quantities of butter or cream into his chocolate. When Mrs Thrale mentioned her dislike of roast goose, because one could smell it all over the house while it was cooking, 'You, madam,' said Johnson, 'have always had your hunger forestalled by indulgence, and do not know the pleasure of smelling one's meat beforehand.' At table he would never talk until he had first taken off the edge of his appetite. Of his physical courage something has been said already: warned while he was bathing that a certain pool was dangerous, he at once swam into it. On his tour to the Hebrides, the boat in which he and Boswell were sailing amongst the islands was caught in a sudden hard blow; Johnson, though he disliked the sea on principle, was the only man on board to remain totally unperturbed. With his physical courage – a quality, as he himself put it, so necessary to maintaining virtue – went a moral courage even more notable. He feared no man, when what he believed to be honourable or true was at stake. There is the instance of his famous letter to James Macpherson, who claimed to have translated the poems of Ossian. Johnson from the first had disbelieved in the existence of the Erse original of this work, and had said so publicly and in print. Macpherson had replied with abuse and threats. Johnson was not intimidated. 'Mr James Macpherson,' he wrote, 'I received your foolish and impudent letter. Any violence offered me I shall do my best to repel; and what I cannot do for myself, the law shall do for me. I hope I shall not be deterred from detecting what I think a cheat by the menaces of a ruffian.

'What would you have me retract? I thought your book an imposture; I think it an imposture still. Your rage I defy. . . . What I hear of your morals inclines me to pay regard not to what you shall say, but to what you shall prove. You may print this if you will. Sam. Johnson.' No doubt there is something of the Old Adam in this, as in his punishment of Osborne, the bookseller; asked by Boswell if the story was true that he had knocked Osborne down in his shop with a folio, 'Sir,' he replied, 'he was impertinent to me, and I beat him. But it was not in his shop; it was in my own chamber.' On both these occasions one seems to catch a glint in Johnson's eye; but one likes him none the less for it. He had a gust for the physical basis of life, and was an enemy to no innocent pleasure. He liked to see others enjoying themselves. Unlike some moralists, he never pretended to despise wealth or the gratifications it can bring. He knew too well what poverty was to sing its praises; and when he ceased to be poor, he never forgot the great mass of mankind who were poor still. To them he was always generous to excess, often emptying his pockets of all they contained, and not caring overmuch if the money was spent on gin and tobacco. In the London of Johnson's day, more than a thousand people died every year of hunger, or of the diseases caused by hunger; it was Johnson's vivid realization of this that made him refuse to grudge the small pleasures which a coin might bring. Finding a woman lying in the street and reduced by vice and hunger to the last extreme of wretchedness, he carried her on his back to his lodging, looked after her with much tenderness for days and did what he could to persuade her to reform her life.

His rough manner was the cloak for the tenderest of hearts. Only when his principles were touched upon the quick could he be roused to anger or scorn, and then no one was a greater master of invective. When Bolingbroke's works were brought out in 1754, edited by David Mallet, Johnson's comment was: 'Sir, he was a scoundrel and a coward: a scoundrel for charging a blunderbuss against religion and morality; a coward, because he had no resolution to fire it off himself, but left half a crown to a beggarly Scotchman to draw the trigger after his death.' Even his love of knocking a man down in argument was followed, often enough, by repentance: at a dinner one day he was moved to call Goldsmith impertinent; later, at the club, the two men met again. 'Dr Goldsmith,' said Johnson, 'something passed today where you and I dined; I ask your pardon.' 'It must be much from you, sir,' Goldsmith answered, 'that I take ill.' Towards all human weakness Johnson was the least censorious of men – he was too vividly conscious of his own. Goldsmith, whom he loved, died £2,000 in debt: 'Was ever poet so trusted before?' was Johnson's comment.

But the real depth of Johnson's tenderness was hardly known even to his friends; for they had not seen his letters

65

to other friends, or his private journal. His house was an asylum for the unfortunate: Mrs Desmoulins, Mrs Williams, Dr Levet, were all supported by him, the last two until they died. Mrs Williams was totally blind; he never failed to drink tea with her in the evening; she would sit up for him, no matter how late he came home. To Mrs Desmoulins and her daughter he gave a room in his house and half a guinea a week. Levet practised as a doctor amongst the very poor, and was probably ignorant; in all his illnesses, Johnson insisted on the attendance of Levet, whatever other doctor was there. 'Levet', he once said, 'is a brutal fellow, but I have a good regard for him, for his brutality is in his manners, not in his mind.' All these dependants – a word he would have refused indignantly to apply to them – he treated with the same courtesy as he used towards the finest gentlemen of the land. All Johnson's charity sprang from the heart; he dreaded the discovery of new countries, lest it should result in conquest and cruelty. He was eloquent on behalf of the Negro slaves. 'Oh I loved Bet Flint,' he exclaimed to Fanny Burney and Mrs Thrale, having just told them that Bet was habitually a slut and a drunkard, and occasionally a thief. Francis, his Negro servant, he sent for four years to school, and would often write to him when away from home, asking after his progress in reading and telling him 'to be a good boy'. He would always go out himself in order to buy oysters (of all things!) for his cat Hodge, lest Francis should be hurt by having to wait upon an animal. He left Francis the bulk of his property when he died. In the days of his own poverty he would put pennies into the hands of children whom he found sleeping on doorsteps in the London streets. 'Remember, my dear darling,' he wrote to Lucy Porter, his stepdaughter, who does not seem to have been a very amiable woman, 'that one of my greatest pleasures is to please you'; and, in another letter on the occasion of his mother's death: 'I should be glad if Kitty will write to me.' Kitty was his mother's old servant; when she was on her deathbed, Johnson visited her. 'Yesterday, at about ten in the morning,' he wrote in his private journal, 'I took my leave for ever of my dear old friend Catherine Chambers. I desired all to withdraw, then told her that we were to part for ever; that, as Christians, we should part with prayer; and that I would, if she was willing, say a short prayer beside her. She expressed great desire to hear me; and held up her poor hands, as she lay in bed, with great fervour, while I prayed, kneeling beside her. . . . I then kissed her. She told me that to part was the greatest pain that she had ever felt, and that she hoped we should meet again in a better place. I expressed, with swelled eyes and great emotion of tenderness, the same hopes. We kissed, and parted. I humbly hope to meet again, and to part no more.' He never, in his long years as a widower, forgot his wife, his 'dear Tetty'; in Paris with the Thrales, twenty-three years after her death, she was in his mind when he went to see the Palais Bourbon. 'As I entered,' he wrote, in one of his little 'paper books', 'my wife was in my mind; she would have been pleased. Having now nobody to please, I am little pleased.' He was markedly kind to children and animals, in an age which, in general, paid scant attention to either. That Johnson was majestic, all the world knows: always majestic in manner, often (but by no means always) majestic in speech; but one need not read deeply in the records of his life to find his companionable and affectionate heart. 'I consider myself', he once complacently remarked to Boswell, 'to be a good-natured fellow.'

Enough has been said of Johnson's constant sickness and secret misery; one should add only that he rarely complained. He was not happy – and saw no reason why he should be. For the weakness which makes a man talk of his distresses he had nothing but contempt. When Mrs Thrale asked him how he did, 'Ready to become a scoundrel, madam,' he answered; 'with a little more spoiling, you will make me a complete rascal.'

Courage and kindliness such as Johnson's were enough to win the affection of all who knew him; but he was not only loved, he was respected: more than that, he became an almost legendary figure while he was yet alive. One famous saying of his, perhaps the most familiar of all his sayings, best exemplifies what is of permanent value in Johnson's thought, whether expressed in his writings or in his talk, and best explains the hold he had over his contemporaries, and continues to have over us: 'clear your *mind* of cant'. Johnson never gave Boswell, or anyone else, better advice. What one says to satisfy social convention may not always matter; what one thinks, is vital to one's own integrity. 'I may call myself your humble servant – I am *not* your humble servant.' 'When a butcher tells you that his heart bleeds for his country, he has, in fact, no uneasy feeling.' That honesty is central in all Johnson's thinking; he was not a subtle or generative thinker, but an eminently sane and practical one. His thought was the thought of ordinary men, but strengthened and clarified, and always fearlessly expressed. He never spoke, or thought, at random; he rarely speculated; his conclusions were invariably drawn from his own direct experience, from what he knew of himself and what he had observed of men. It is this that gives his talk, and much of his writing, its astonishing vitality. His dislike of speculation sometimes led him into error, as when he thought to refute Berkeley's theory of matter by striking his foot against a stone. But this was the defect of his quality, and is amply compensated by the refreshing candour and sovereign honesty of his mind. When the company began to talk one day of free will (that subject which Milton has told us puzzled even the angels in hell), 'Sir,' Johnson irritably exclaimed, 'we *know* the will is free, and there's an end on't'.

Similarly, as a critic, Johnson brought literature to the test of real life and actual experience. 'Does this author', he seems to say, 'write sense or nonsense? Is what he tells us true? If so, let us commend him; if not, we will better employ our time in reading somebody else.' His judgements are as uncompromising as they are often witty; writing of Gray (whom he never liked; 'Gray', he once said, 'is a dull fellow: dull in his closet, dull in company, dull everywhere. He was dull in a new way and that made many people think him great.') he comes to mention his *Eton College* ode, and on the appeal in that poem to Father Thames to tell

> who chase the rolling circle's speed
> or urge the flying ball

he comments: 'His supplication to Father Thames to tell him who drives the hoop or tosses the ball, is useless and puerile. Father Thames has no better means of knowing than himself.' No doubt Johnson chuckled as he wrote that sentence: nevertheless, he was fundamentally in earnest about it. The criticism was in his manner, springing as it did from his belief that even poets should not be allowed to write nonsense. The belief may be somewhat restrictive, but it is a wholesome one. It makes all Johnson's best writings, as Boswell said of his *Rambler* essays, 'bark and steel for the mind'. One may incidentally observe that the couple of sentences quoted above go some way to refute the common belief that Johnson always wrote *Johnsonese*: the manner of them is almost colloquial in its lightness and ease – and the same can be said of much of Johnson's later work, especially of his *Lives of the Poets*, which he wrote in his old age to please himself, and not as a hack 'writing for bread'.

Johnson was a moralist, and he lived in a moralistic

age. Readers in the eighteenth century seem to have had as much entertainment in reading moral essays and sermons as we have today in reading fiction – and the practical effect in either case has probably been about the same. Johnson, however, brought his ethics, like his literary criticism, to the test of experience. He knew men, and, above all, he knew himself. 'A fallible being', he would say, 'will fail somewhere', and he knew, no man better, his own fallibility. Deeply and sincerely religious, his mind, in hours of solitude, was perpetually occupied in the struggle to conquer his faults. If one read nothing he wrote except his journal – his *Prayers and Meditations* – one might conclude that this man, who got through so great a mass of work and delighted with his talk every man and woman of culture and intellect in London society over a period of fifty years, had led a life of failure and futile irresolution: 'From the earliest time almost that I can remember, I have been forming schemes of a better life. I have done nothing. The need of doing, therefore, is pressing, since the time of doing is short. O God, grant me to resolve aright, and to keep my resolutions, for Jesus Christ's sake.' Again and again the entries in the journal are in the same strain, self-accusations of lethargy, self-indulgence, and blunted purposes, and always accompanied by an earnest prayer for reformation. He was haunted by a sense of sin and the fear of hell – and of death, which might be the gateway to it. One may call this morbid, if one will; indeed, it was so: it sprang, in part at any rate, from the diseased body he was born with, and the 'black dog' (his own phrase) which he never succeeded in shaking from his back. It was akin to the queer little superstitious habits which Boswell observed in him, the counting of paces to his door, to be sure of reaching the step with a particular foot, right or left as the case might be – perhaps even to his mysterious practice of collecting orange-peel. It was the dark side of his triumphant rationalism. But it is also, for us, the measure of his humility. Amongst his equals he was as proud as Lucifer; he exulted in his intellectual superiority; in the battle of wits he loved, when the mood was on him, to bang his opponent into dumbness; yet no man ever had a humbler or more compassionate heart.

His statue in Westminster Abbey shows him standing, and dressed – inappropriately — in a toga – like Cicero. It is better to remember him as Boswell described him for us in his rusty brown suit and small black wig, sitting in his chair with his head to one side towards his right shoulder and shaking it in a tremulous manner, as he moved his body backwards and forwards, and rubbed his left knee with the palm of his hand. So, with his friends, he would sit and talk and drink his tea until the small hours, 'sometimes giving half a whistle, sometimes making his tongue play backwards from the roof of his mouth, as if clucking like a hen, and sometimes protruding it against his upper gums in front, as if pronouncing quickly under his breath, *too, too, too*: all this accompanied sometimes with a thoughtful look, but more frequently with a smile.'

Nelson

ALL the saints, and a few of the poets – Milton and
Wordsworth amongst them – have had a moment of
vision in which their life's work has been revealed to them
and claimed once and for all the dedication of their
spirits. The moment has been for them an inspiration to
attempt, even if not to suceed, and they have lived by the
breath of it. Amongst men of action this sort of inspiration must be rare; but it came to Nelson, and is one of the
first things to remember if one wishes to understand the
peculiar radiance which surrounds his brief and brilliant
career. At the age of eighteen, homeward bound from the
East Indies in the frigate *Dolphin*, half-paralysed and reduced to a skeleton by malarial fever and almost at the
point of death, when all his hopes were vanished and the
cold darkness of oblivion seemed about to close over him
for ever, he was suddenly aware of what he later described as a 'radiant orb' suspended before his mind's
eye and beckoning him onward. Gone in a moment was
his resignation to failure and death; 'a glow of patriotism' – as he afterwards put it – 'was kindled within me,
and presented my King and Country as my patron. My
mind exulted in the idea. "Well then," I exclaimed, "I
will be a hero, and confiding in Providence, I will brave
every danger." ' The words are commonplace, almost
trite; but the experience they describe was genuine and
profound. It was akin to the experience of the mystics
and the poets, and by it Nelson, a practical seaman who
lived his life amongst hardships, violence, and bloodshed, is admitted to their company. He was a dedicated
spirit – to use the phrase which Wordsworth used of

himself one memorable morning, when he knew for the
first time, and finally, that he must give himself to poetry;
and by a similar inspiration Nelson, too, foresaw the
future in the instant. At that moment, as he lay so near
death in the frigate's cabin, he was *converted* to life. The
word is not inappropriate; for it was no mere conscious
decision that he made to get the better of circumstance:
it was something given, making him the instrument of a
power which flowed mysteriously in on him from the far
sources of life. That youthful experience is the key to his
quality and character. Other men in the splendid succession of English seamen have been as brave, and almost
as successful, as Nelson; but Nelson's rapt abandonment and self-forgetfulness in the hour of danger have
no parallel, and have caught the imagination of the
English people in the strongest toil. His courage was
not a dogged, but an inspired, courage; he embraced
danger and death like a lover, and exulted in both. When
one thinks of his great naval actions, one is apt to forget
the months, sometimes the years, of waiting, the careful
and efficient planning, the minute orders issued to his
fleet, and to see only the small rapt figure sailing to almost
certain death with the ecstasy of a saint adoring his God.
Moreover, the same visionary experience is the key not
only to Nelson's greatness, but to the curious littleness
which accompanied it like its shadow. No man's inspiration is constant; the glow cools, before it is fanned to life
again, and then the possessor of it looks with a sort of
wonder at the man he was, as if that man were not himself, but another. Reading the *Tale of a Tub* years after it
was written, 'What a genius', Swift exclaimed, 'I had
when I wrote that book!' In the same way Nelson, in the
long level stretches of his life between the peaks, seems at
times to detach himself from what he was, and what he
knows he will again be when the tide of occasion serves,
and to look at that other self with the admiration of a

stranger. He speaks, and even writes, of his own courage with the vanity of a schoolboy; he grumbles at being given 'only' a barony after the battle of the Nile; he fills his house at Merton with pictures of himself and records of his victories; he delights in being feted and admired; he is greedy for flattery and praise, and wears his orders and his stars in season and out of season; he harps upon the theme of honour and duty more than an Englishman has need to do. Again and again he seems to be acting a part, and some may wonder, watching him, why it is that this vain man has won the chief place in his country's love, rather than the grim, sardonic Wellington, his great contemporary, who fought no less nobly and did not care a rap for applause, or dour old Captain Cook, who went quietly about his immense and perilous adventures without a single thought for the figure he might cut in the eyes of the world – and never deserted his Elizabeth. Nevertheless we need not wonder; the instinct was right which gave the most spectacular memorial in London not to Wellington or Cook, or to Howe or Hood, or Jervis or Rodney, but to Nelson; it was right, because it marks our recognition not only of the outstanding part he played in saving England from the worst danger which ever threatened her before the twentieth century, but also of his essential quality as man and leader, the inspired and mystical element in his character, which had so profound an influence upon all who came into contact with him, and continues to command the special allegiance of a people whom other nations wrongly suppose to have won their position in the world only by coolheadedness, common sense, and practical ability.

It is necessary to stress this aspect of Nelson at the out-set, because without regard to it no one can understand his character and career. Nelson was the poet in action; in his grandest moments he ceased to belong to this world and entered a realm as visionary as Shelley's; he turned the bitter and beastly business of war into an innocent ecstasy, and those who fought under him moved, for the moment, within the same circle of light. They could not escape its radiance. Former grumblers and mutineers were reduced to instant obedience, and worshipped him; the grim Collingwood, when the famous signal was run up on board the *Victory* before the ships engaged at Trafalgar, muttered to his lieutenant that he wished Nelson would stop signalling for once – for didn't everyone know what he was to do? But the instant the message was read to him, he had it proclaimed to every man aboard, and was answered with a cheer. He had yielded to Nelson's spell. Nelson was, in his great moments, spell-bound and spell-binding. 'There is an electric fire', wrote Keats, 'in human nature tending to purify – so that among these human creatures there is continually some birth of new heroism.' There was an electric fire in Nelson, and his acts, the smallest as well as the greatest, were purified by it and redeemed from being mere attitudes. Many people have called him theatrical; but he was not theatrical, for even when he seems to be playing a part, that part is in essence himself and springs straight and spontaneously from what he is. No English officer but Nelson could have presented himself immediately after the action of Cape St Vincent, his face blackened with powder, his clothes in rags, and half his hat shot away, upon the quarterdeck of his commander-in-chief; but for Nelson the act was wholly in character, and old Sir John Jervis, by no means an imaginative man, was instantly captured by the spirit of it and hugged Nelson in his arms. Nelson had no need to act, or to pretend to be other than he was; if he trod the stage gallantly, and sometimes with a flourish, it was always the stage of life. A theatrical man is a false man; but nothing but an essential and demonic reality could have made common men and women, when Nelson left his inn to join the *Victory* in Spithead before Trafalgar, fall on their knees as he passed to ask his blessing. That he enjoyed such scenes, and even courted them (though not upon that occasion) is nothing to the purpose. But one must not forget, on the other hand, that he was also a superb practical seaman; he learned his business in the hard way, going to sea as a child of twelve and serving in all sorts of ships in every part of the world, from the tropics to the ice-bound north. His knowledge of every branch of his profession was exact, his grasp of detail unsurpassed by any other sea-officer of his time. When he was a young captain of twenty-four and had never been in a fleet action, Lord Hood told the Duke of Clarence that, if he wanted information on naval tactics, Nelson was the man to go to. The 'Nelson touch' (his own phrase) was only the climax of his great actions; all of them were planned beforehand in minutest detail, with scrupulous regard for all possible variation in the prevailing conditions when the decisive moment should come. He cared for his men with an almost fatherly concern, knowing them all by name and character and never forgetting a face; they were of the same stuff as Wellington's men, but for Nelson they were never 'the scum of the earth', but always 'my poor brave fellows' – as his midshipmen were his 'children'. All gave him their devotion; Nelson's discipline was strict and impeccable, but his ships were happy ships. He hated punishment (the savage floggings of those days) and used it sparingly, and suffered when it was unavoidably administered. Off Cadiz in the *Theseus*, which had been heavily involved in the recent mutiny at the Nore, a paper was dropped upon the quarterdeck one night: 'Success attend Admiral Nelson!' The writing ran; 'God bless Captain Miller! We thank them for the officers they have placed over us. We are happy and comfortable, and will shed every drop of blood in our veins to support them, and the name of the *Theseus* shall be immortalized as high as the *Captain's*. SHIP'S COMPANY.' The ship's company which subscribed to that message had been known as the worst in the English fleet. It is a touching tribute to the personal ascendancy of a commander who had no need to enforce obedience through fear.

Nelson never fully recovered from the attack of fever which nearly killed him at the age of eighteen. The after-effects of it were a burden for the rest of his life, or would have been a burden, had he paused to attend to them. He was seldom free from pain; but the spirit in his frail and increasingly battered little body was like a bright sword in a rusty sheath. He gave himself no rest – except for one period of six years, doubtless the unhappiest of his life, when he had no ship and was forced to remain ashore, fretting his heart out. In stature he was small and slightly built, with fair hair, eyes blue and friendly, and wide, sensitive mouth; the portraits of him are tantalizing, each one being different in effect from all the rest; but the two death-masks show us his features. When the masks were taken, he had been dead six weeks and pickled in brandy; but, though the light is gone from the face, both masks are beautiful. They show a curious resemblance to the poet Keats – who also had his 'radiant orb' to follow, and whose courage, though of a very different order, was not less in degree than Nelson's own. Opening his Spenser one day, Keats came upon the lines:

> The noble heart that harbours virtuous thought,
> And is with child of glorious great intent,
> Shall never rest until it forth have brought
> The eternal brood of glory excellent;

The words would have fired Nelson too. Keats, on one memorable occasion, found it 'rich to die', and precisely the same mood of exaltation and self-surrender was Nelson's every time his ship went into action. The electric fire in men has, fortunately, as many shapes as Proteus; but it is the same fire.

Nelson was born on 29 September 1758, in the parsonage house at the Norfolk village of Burnham Thorpe, where his father, the Rev. Edmund Nelson, was rector. He was the sixth child of his parents, and his mother died when he was nine, leaving the rector to bring up a family of eight children, which he did with frugality and strictness. Mrs Edmund Nelson's grandmother was a sister of Sir Robert Walpole, and Nelson was christened Horatio to mark the connexion with that distinguished family. Of his early childhood nothing is known, except that he attended the High School in Norwich and another school at North Walsham; there are, indeed, legends about his earliest years, believed by those who care to believe such things: great men have always been a cause of myth-making, and such stories as how Nelson asked his grandmama what fear was because he had never seen it, are probably no truer than the story of how Cyrus the Great played at kings with the other village boys and beat the son of Artembares for disobedience – and are certainly not so good. When he was twelve years old, he read in a newspaper that his uncle, Captain Maurice Suckling, after a spell ashore on half pay, had been given a ship again; Nelson had not been intended for the sea, but this piece of news caught his fancy and he at once persuaded his father to ask the Captain to take him aboard. 'What', came the answer, 'has poor Horatio done that he, above all the rest, should be sent to rough it out at sea? But let him come . . . a cannon ball may knock off his head and provide for him at once.' So the boy went, and was introduced to the midshipmen's berth in the *Raisonnable*, 64 guns, lying at Chatham. It was a heavy change from the Norfolk parsonage; he was, and remained through life, as an old friend testified, a 'thorough clergyman's son', and there was doubtless much in his new surroundings to distress him. In later life, on being told by an officer that he, too, had entered the service at the age of twelve, Nelson was heard to mutter, 'much too young'. He must, in that moment, have remembered the *Raisonnable*, the cramped quarters, the harsh discipline, the unwholesome and revolting food, the strangeness of it all after the warmth and kindliness of home. Nelson always put himself out in later years to be kind to his midshipmen; once when he was a Captain, and found that one of them was scared of going aloft (and the horrid backward incline of the futtock shrouds was enough to scare any boy), 'Sir,' he said to him, 'I am going a race to the masthead, and trust that I shall meet you there'.

He was not long in the *Raisonnable*. Thanks partly to the help and influence of his uncle, who was fond of him, and partly to his own quickness and determination, his advance was unusually rapid. There is not space in a brief account to trace it step by step; it must suffice to record that Suckling sent him on a voyage to the West Indies in a merchant vessel, to learn the elements of navigation and seamanship, and, on his return, put him in the cutter which was attached to the Commanding Officer's ship at Chatham. In the cutter he had a chance of getting to know the London river from Chatham to the Tower, and the intricate pilotage of the Thames estuary, a maze of shoals and complicated tidal streams, through the Swin channel to the North Foreland. It was fine training for a boy, and he remained grateful for it all his life. When he was fifteen, only a month or two after Cook in the *Resolution* had crossed the Antarctic Circle for the first time in the world's history, he joined an expedition which was fitting out to explore the Arctic seas. Boys had been officially banned, but the young Nelson managed to get a berth as coxswain to Captain Lutwidge in the bomb-ketch *Carcase*. It was not an important expedition; scientifically it achieved nothing, but for Nelson it was more experience, and gave him the pleasing opportunity of trying to kill a polar bear with the butt-end of his musket. Immediately on returning home he was transferred to a frigate bound for the East Indies; in her, he served a part of his time as able-seaman – a foretop-man, like Melville's Billy Budd. The cruise ended three years later with the bout of fever, which nearly finished him. It was during his voyage home that he was 'converted to life'. That inconspicuous and silent drama, played in the small, dark, comfortless cabin on board the frigate *Dolphin* between a sick boy and his own soul, was to be of incalculable import to England's destiny. A week or two after reaching home he was well enough to go to sea again, this time as acting-lieutenant in the *Worcester*, and before the year was out he passed his examinations for lieutenant, and was off at once for the West Indies in the frigate *Lowestoft*. On this voyage he had his first taste of fighting – a small affair, but Nelson always remembered it, and it is not without significance in the development of his character. At this time (1777) American privateers were interfering with British trade in the islands, and British ships had orders to retaliate. An American having struck her flag to the *Lowestoft*, in a gale of wind and heavy sea, the first lieutenant hesitated to board her. 'Have I no officer', cried Captain Locker, 'who will board the prize?' The Master at once volunteered, but Nelson, as his senior, claimed the privilege for himself and leapt into the boat. No doubt most good officers would have done the same, but the little act is a good instance of the extreme swiftness of decision which, combined with extreme tenacity of purpose, characterized Nelson throughout his life. In the following year he was transferred to the flagship of Admiral Sir Peter Parker, by whose good offices, and helped no doubt by the fact that he was a nephew of Captain Suckling, now Comptroller of the Navy, he was promoted to his first command. The ship was the brig *Badger*, and Nelson was twenty years of age.

In 1779 his rapid rise in his profession was nearly cut short by a second serious illness. Spain had entered the war on the side of France, and Nelson volunteered for the command of the naval part of a crack-brained combined operation, which would be better forgotten were it not for Nelson's share in it. The plan was to force a way up the San Juan river in Nicaragua, seize Granada and, having thus cut Spanish Central America in two, to open a way into the Pacific. It was Drake's dream over again, but, though greater resources and much greater knowledge were available than in Drake's day, the venture met with no more success. Wretchedly conceived and inadequately equipped, starting at the wrong time of year when the rainy season had already begun, it was doomed from the outset. Of Nelson's two hundred seamen only ten survived. Nelson himself worked like a black and appears to have enjoyed himself, while his health lasted. 'I want words', wrote Colonel Polson, who was in command of the five hundred soldiers who composed the land force, 'to express the obligations I owe that gentleman; he was the first upon every service, whether by night or by day.' Fortunately he was recalled to take command of another ship, before the dismal end; but the old fever had taken violent hold of him, and he had to be carried ashore when he reached Jamaica. Here he was nursed back to a kind of health by Lady Parker, the Admiral's wife, and by Lady Parker's little daughter, who alone could persuade him to swallow his medicines. We shall see him on other occasions, too, led captive by the very young; his nature, at bottom passionate and tender, had few defences: that was why children loved him, as it was also one of the secrets of his power.

For the next couple of years after a brief rest at home, Nelson was first in the Baltic and then in North American waters with the *Albemarle*. Here he met Prince William Henry, afterwards King William IV, who was serving as a midshipman in the *Barfleur*, Lord Hood's flagship. The two at once became, and always remained, friends. Admiral Hood also saw the young captain's quality, and was a powerful influence in his advancement; Nelson had still taken no part in a fleet action, but genius is not easily hid, and he was already recognized as a rising star.

At the end of the American war Nelson returned to England and remained ashore for nearly a year. The interval is important for one small but revelatory incident – Nelson fell in love, and appears to have been refused. The statement has a commonplace air, but for a man of Nelson's temperament it was not a commonplace event. Moreover, it helps to explain the foolish marriage which he soon afterwards made. He was now twenty-five and had already been rescued by a friend from a marriage which would have been more foolish even than the one he actually contracted. The woman, a Miss Andrews, was the daughter of a clergyman, living in France, whither Nelson had gone in a vain attempt to learn French, and perhaps to seek some outlet for the suppressed emotional fire which always threatened to consume him. It is one of the little ironies of human character that young men most capable of love should almost invariably be ignorant just where it most behoves them to be wise. When Nelson really fell in love, it was, unhappily for himself, and still more unhappily for his wife, finally and for ever. He gave himself to love with the same ruthless abandonment as that with which he gave himself to his work.

After his visit to France he went to sea again, hoping to forget his trouble. While stationed in the Leeward Islands, he found some comfort in the friendship of a

woman older than himself; she was Mrs Moutray, wife
of the Commissioner at Antigua – 'my sweet amiable
friend', Nelson called her. But she returned to England
and left him desolate. 'I went once up the hill', he wrote,
'to look at the spot where I spent more happy days than
in any one spot in the world.' Then, immediately afterwards, he met Fanny Nisbet, and married her. Mrs
Nisbet, niece of John Herbert, President of the island of
Nevis, was a young widow, with a son three years old.
Nelson appears to have been fond of her, but there is
little doubt that he did not love her. He 'esteemed' her –
his own word, which occurs in his letters all too often.
The marriage might have been well enough for some
men; it was not for Nelson; but – he could not live alone,
and his goose-love was, in his restless fancy, a swan. It
was a bad day for both of them when Prince William
Henry gave away the bride on 12 March 1787. In the
following July the two returned to England with the
baby – Josiah – and settled in the old parsonage house.
Nelson was fond of the child; he had made its acquaintance before ever he met Fanny, and was discovered one
morning by Fanny's father playing with it under the
dining-room table. Fanny herself was to give him no
children.

For the next six years, while the peace lasted, Nelson
was ashore. He could not get a ship. The reason was that
during the time he had spent in the Leeward Islands he
had caused some embarrassment to his seniors and made
himself in many ways unpopular. America, at the end of
the War of Independence, had become a foreign country;
but her ships continued to trade with the British-owned
islands without any of the restrictions to which foreign
shipping was subject. By the islanders themselves the
illegal practice, being profitable, was winked at; Nelson,
however, had no intention of allowing it to continue, and
at once set to work to stop it. Protests poured in. Nelson

was ordered by his Admiral to desist; he ignored the order. He sought an interview with the Governor of the islands, General Shirley, and tried to get his support. 'Old generals', said Sir Thomas, 'are not in the habit of taking advice from young gentlemen.' 'Sir,' Nelson replied, 'I am as old as the Prime Minister of England, and think myself as capable of commanding one of His Majesty's ships as that minister is of governing the State.' It was an uncompromising answer – like Drake before him, Nelson was not an easy subordinate. So the years in England dragged on and Nelson remained unemployed. He dabbled in politics and tried to interest himself in country pursuits, gardening and shooting – in the latter, it seems, causing more danger to his companions than to bird or beast, for he would carry his gun at full cock and fire from the hip the instant any game appeared. Fanny was an affectionate and dutiful wife, but for her, too, it was a sad change from the luxury and comfort she had known in the Governor's house in Nevis; for Nelson himself the light had gone out of things; his radiant orb had paled. Perhaps if there had been children, his esteem for Fanny might have warmed into love; but there were none. At last, on 11 February 1793, war was declared against revolutionary France. It was Nelson's opportunity. The Admiralty knew his quality: they had looked at him askance during the years of peace, but in war he was indispensable. When he stepped aboard the *Agamemnon* – one of the fine ships built at Buckler's Hard on the Beaulieu river in Hampshire – his spirits went up with a rush. He was at home again.

From 1793 to 1805 Nelson's is the foremost name in English history. It was during these years that England finally established her supremacy at sea, without which she could never have won the war against Napoleon, and it was Nelson's genius that played by far the greatest part in giving her that supremacy. The *Agamemnon* was ordered to the Mediterranean to join the squadron under Lord Hood. Nelson was delighted with his new ship, and with all on board; 'the finest 64 in the service', he called her in a letter to his wife, and added that 'with a good ship and a good ship's company we can come to no harm'. Such generous admiration was typical of him; one reason why he was served as no other commander was served by both officers and men was that he assumed as a matter of course that everyone would do his best. To be trusted has made many a man worthy of trust: and this Nelson instinctively knew, and acted upon the knowledge. That, and the contagious fire of his own spirit, was what welded any force that he commanded into a single whole with a single purpose – into what he himself called, in the beautifully apt and famous phrase which he borrowed from Shakespeare, a 'band of brothers'. But four years were yet to pass before that phrase was used by him, and three before he was engaged in a major fleet action. Meanwhile, as in the abortive expedition in Nicaragua, but with better success, he was to serve again on land. This time the scene was Corsica, where the French were still in possession of three towns, Bastia, San Fiorenzo, and Calvi. It was during the siege of Calvi that Nelson lost the sight of his right eye, being struck by dirt and splinters thrown up by a cannon-ball which pitched near him. The wound kept him out of action only for twenty-four hours. It is sometimes forgotten that both Nelson's serious wounds, the blinding of his eye and the loss of his right arm, were received not at sea, but on land. The second – the shattering of his elbow by grape-shot – occurred three years later during the night attempt to carry the town of Santa Cruz in Teneriffe, where it was thought that the Spanish treasure-ships from the West Indies would try to find refuge. A year before this, on 14 February 1797, occurred the first naval engagement on a great scale in which

Nelson was involved. His genius at once came into its own. Hitherto he had been recognized inside his profession as a coming man, but people at home knew little or nothing of him. After the battle of Cape St Vincent his name became a legend.

In the Mediterranean and in Italy things had been going badly for England. The French were sweeping forward on land; Admiral Hotham, Commander-in-Chief of the Mediterranean fleet, had proved inactive and over-cautious; the island outposts, Corsica and Elba, held by the British, had been abandoned; the Austrians had shown themselves useless and incompetent allies; at the end of 1796 Spain entered the war on the side of France. Happily for England, and for Nelson himself, Hotham had been superseded at the beginning of the same year by Sir John Jervis, who was a man after Nelson's own heart, and at once put a new spirit into the fleet. He was well aware that a victory for England against her new enemy Spain was vitally important. He did not have long to wait for his chance. At dawn on February 14th the Spanish fleet of twenty-seven sail of the line was sighted, heading eastward across the bows of the British squadron of fifteen. The Spaniards were straggled out, with a gap of some eight miles between the leading group of ships and those which were bringing up the rear. Jervis took his squadron in line-ahead straight for the gap. The Spanish commander, seeing his fleet cut in two, ordered his windward division to turn north, perhaps with the intention of getting round the rear of the British line, perhaps in an attempt to avoid battle; upon this, Jervis signalled his ships to tack in succession and engage. The leading ship was the *Culloden*, commanded by Troubridge; she immediately went about and pursued the rearmost Spaniards. Nelson, in the *Captain*, which was third from the rear of the English line, seeing that if Jervis's order to tack in succession were obeyed, the battle would develop into a mere rearguard action and nothing decisive be accomplished, made one of his instant and characteristic decisions. He broke the line, put the *Captain* about, and flung her across the path of the half-dozen leading Spaniards – amongst them the *Santissima Trinidad* of 126 guns. Disobedience is properly deprecated in the fighting services, but Sir John Jervis was man enough to see that Nelson was, in this instance, right. Without a moment's delay he signalled Collingwood in the *Excellent* to support the *Captain*. After nearly an hour of close fighting Nelson found himself alongside the Spanish *San Nicolas*; the *Captain*'s wheel was shot away, her foremast gone by the board, and she was pretty well out of control. Collingwood, on his way to her support, had forced two Spanish ships to strike, but, seeing the dangerous condition of the *Captain*, abandoned his prizes and, coming within a biscuit-throw of the *San Nicolas*, poured a broadside into her. Half torn to pieces, she luffed, and fell foul of her neighbour, the *San Josef*, a great three-decker of 112 guns. Nelson gave the order to grapple, and the three ships – Nelson's *Captain* and the two Spaniards *San Nicolas* and *San Josef* – were locked together. Nelson called for boarders and was instantly answered. Captain Berry, followed by many more, climbed out along the spritsail yard and leapt aboard; a marine smashed a window in the *San Nicolas*'s quarter-gallery with the butt of his musket and jumped through. Nelson followed him. Together they burst the cabin doors and chased the Spaniards on to the quarterdeck. Berry was already there, and the Spanish ensign was coming down. Then from the towering *San Josef*, close alongside, a volley of musket-shot killed seven of the English seamen, and once again Nelson called for boarders. He, with Berry, was the first to scramble into the main-chains of the *San Josef*, and, as he hove himself on to her deck, he shouted his favourite war-cry of

'Westminster Abbey or victory!' The *San Josef* surrendered. The surviving Spanish ships made for Cadiz, where they were blockaded by the British.

It had been Nelson's day; but he would have no praise which was not equally accorded to Troubridge and Collingwood. Recognizing not only the gallantry, but the generosity of Collingwood in leaving his prizes to come to the *Captain*'s assistance, he wrote to him after the battle: 'My dearest friend, – "A friend in need is a friend indeed" was never more truly verified than by your most noble and gallant conduct yesterday in sparing the *Captain* from further loss'; to which 'dear Coll' (as Nelson so often called him in his letters) gruffly replied that 'it added very much to the satisfaction which I felt in thumping the Spaniards that I released you a little'. The victory was timely and notable, but by no means complete – for that, England had to wait until Nelson himself was in command. After the action Jervis was made Earl St Vincent, and Nelson a K.B.; at the same time his regular promotion followed, so that he was now Rear-Admiral Sir Horatio Nelson, K.B. He was thirty-nine.

In July of the same year occurred the unsuccessful attempt upon Teneriffe. As always, Nelson's plan of attack was minutely worked out, but it was defeated by weather and the tides. One incident of this unfortunate expedition is especially memorable: Nelson, his right arm nearly torn off by grape-shot, was being rowed from the harbour mole back to his ship *Theseus*. The night was dark, and the first ship the boat's crew reached happened to be the frigate *Seahorse*. Captain Fremantle, her commander, by the curious custom of those days had his wife aboard, and Fremantle himself was still ashore in the town, whether alive or dead Nelson did not know. The boat's crew wished to put Nelson on board, to get him medical relief without delay, but Nelson refused. 'I would rather die', he said, 'than let Mrs Fremantle see me in this state, when I can give her no news of her husband.' So he was rowed on to the *Theseus*, where his arm was immediately amputated, close to the shoulder. Three days later he was sitting up in his cabin writing to Earl St Vincent – the first of the many admirably legible letters written with his left hand. A few weeks afterwards he sailed for England in the *Seahorse* – together with Fremantle, who had also been seriously wounded in the right arm. Before the year was out, he was promised another ship, and in April 1798 sailed in the *Vanguard* to join Lord St Vincent's fleet, which was still blockading the Spaniards in Cadiz.

The French fleet was in Toulon; it was known to the British that large numbers of transports and troops were in process of assembling there, but where and when Napoleon would strike was anybody's guess. St Vincent's first action when Nelson joined him in the *Vanguard* was to send him to Toulon with two other ships of the line and three frigates, to try to discover what the intentions of the French might be; then, on the arrival of reinforcements from England, he dispatched ten more of his best ships under Troubridge to join him. Nelson thus had sufficient force to deal with the French fleet when it ventured out of harbour. Unfortunately, however, he missed it. A heavy gale before the arrival of Troubridge with his squadron did serious damage to the *Vanguard*, and she was forced to spend four days refitting in a Sardinian port; at Toulon itself the weather was moderate, and the French seized the opportunity of getting to sea. Napoleon was with them, and nobody knew whither they were bound. The hunt was up – 'My lord,' Nelson wrote to St Vincent, 'I have only to assure you I will bring the French fleet to action the moment I can lay hands on them. Till then, Adieu.' Nelson believed – and was correct in his belief – that Napoleon's destination was Egypt; but he could not be sure, and his frigates, the 'eyes of the fleet', had parted company in the gale and never rejoined him. He sailed south for Naples, then on to Sicily, where he got news that the French had seized Malta six days before, and had at once put to sea again – with a westerly wind. That pointed to Egypt, so to Egypt Nelson set his course. He had been misinformed in Sicily about dates; the French had left Malta four days later than he had been told, and the British fleet actually passed them during a night of fog without seeing them. De Brueys, the French admiral, was sailing east, to make the Cretan coast before bearing south for Alexandria; Nelson took the direct route, and reached the port before him. Finding the French were not there, he was off again without delay – first to the Syrian coast, then to Crete (which de Brueys had just left), then back to Sicily. 'If they are above water,' he wrote to St Vincent, 'I will find them out, and bring them to battle.' From Sicily he sailed to Greece, and there, at last, got definite news: nearly a month before the French fleet had been sighted, sailing from Crete south-easterly for Egypt. Nelson was too late to catch Napoleon and his troops; but he would make no more mistakes with de Brueys. He set his course under all sail for Alexandria. On August 1st, at about three o'clock in the afternoon, Captain Hood signalled from the *Zealous* that he could see the French fleet at anchor in Aboukir Bay. Nelson replied with a signal to all ships to prepare for battle, and then, to the surprise of his officers, ordered dinner. For days past he had had neither food nor sleep; now, he was calm and happy, and, bright in his mind's eye, his star was glowing.

The French ships, thirteen sail of the line, were anchored stem to stern along the whole curve of the little bay, leaving insufficient room, in de Brueys' opinion, for any hostile ship to pass between the windward end of the line and the shoals off what is now called Nelson's Island.

Indeed, so confident was the French admiral of the impossibility of this being done, that he had not had his ships cleared for action on their port (or landward) sides. Nelson, however, at once perceived that where there was space for a ship to swing at her anchors, there was also space for another ship to pass. Upon this, to the consternation of the French, he acted. The sun was almost on the horizon as the English fleet, strung out, approached the bay before a light top-gallant breeze from the north-west. The leading vessels made straight for the narrow gap and passed in-shore of the French line. As the sun set the first shots were fired. One after another five ships slipped through and dropped their anchors, each close aboard a Frenchman; then Nelson in the *Vanguard* led the remainder – all but the *Culloden* which had run aground on the shoal – down the outside of the French, so as to envelop the windward section of their line and overwhelm it by superior force. Like all naval actions in the days of the wooden ships, the range was fearfully close: often so close – a few yards only – that the flame from a gun's muzzle would scorch the sides of the ship it was fired at. Darkness fell; and by nine o'clock the first five ships in de Brueys' line had surrendered. Nelson, engaged in a duel to the death with the *Spartiate*, was wounded again just before she was silenced: a flap of skin, torn from his forehead, fell over his eye, blinding him. The doctor patched him up and ordered him to rest – in a dark little store-room below decks. It was a futile order: Nelson promptly sent for his secretary and began to dictate dispatches. Then, seeing that the man's hand was shaking, he seized the pen, and wrote himself. At that instant Captain Berry came to report that the French flagship, *Orient*, was in flames. Nelson hurried on deck, and a few minutes later, with a tremendous explosion, the *Orient* blew up. De Brueys had already been killed. In the small hours of the morning a final end was made of the French resistance. Of their thirteen ships of the line and four frigates, nine had been taken and four either blown up or sunk; the remaining four escaped. The English fleet, though badly battered, was intact; when daylight came it lay scattered on the water of the bay, with half the crews fallen into an exhausted sleep beside their guns. Napoleon's army had indeed landed in Egypt – but it could not return. France had no fleet left to bring it home again. British naval power in the Mediterranean was restored. The Battle of the Nile was one of the decisive events in the long war. The curious in such things may like to remember that at this moment of time, in a quiet Somersetshire hamlet, another work of genius was coming to fruition: Wordsworth was putting the finishing touches to the *Lyrical Ballads*, a small book which was destined to work upon the spirit of England more subtly but hardly less powerfully than the guns at Aboukir. Jane Austen, too, was smiling in happy irony over the last pages of *Northanger Abbey*.

There were great rejoicings, not only in England but in all the Mediterranean countries, at the news of the victory of Aboukir. Nelson was granted by Parliament a pension of £2,000 a year and raised to the peerage, with the title of Baron Nelson of the Nile. Naples was the first to hear the news, and it was to Naples that Nelson himself went as soon as his ships were made fit to sail. A small squadron was left to blockade the Egyptian coast, and the remainder of the fleet, with some of the prizes, sent to rejoin Lord St Vincent. Nelson was ill; the anxiety and nervous strain of the long pursuit, the lightning climax, and his customary refusal properly to nurse his wound, had told upon a constitution which had never since boyhood been robust. His body was wasted, his face haggard and drawn, and he vomited continually; but he could not, or would not, rest. It was in this condition that in Naples, *en fête* to welcome him, he was received into the household of Sir William Hamilton, the British Ambassador, and of his wife, Lady Hamilton. He had met the Hamiltons once before, five years previously, on a brief visit to Naples, and had parted from both with mutual affection and esteem. Emma Hamilton was a young woman of humble origin, the familiar pattern of whose past, before she married Sir William, had in it as much to pity as to blame. She was beautiful, intelligent, accomplished, and not without fineness of feeling, in spite of a manner at its best flamboyant, at its worst a little vulgar; the noblest thing in a life not noble was her love of Nelson. Sir William, who was on the wrong side of sixty, was compliant, and turned a blind eye. As for Nelson himself, it is absurd, and perhaps impertinent, to look around, as many biographers have done, for censure or excuse. The facts are sufficient. A great chapter in his life had been triumphantly brought to its close; the reaction, mental and physical, was violent; sick and exhausted, deprived for long months of the tenderness which his nature craved, he was nursed and cosseted by Emma Hamilton with the flattery he loved and – soon – with a passion she made no attempt to conceal. As Nelson counted no risks in the service of his country, so he was no diplomat in love; he surrendered at once and for ever. There was a star, one cannot but feel, which for a long time in Nelson's firmament had

swung blind in unascended majesty;

and Emma now assumed her throne. The star was hers; and for the remaining seven years of Nelson's life it shone for him, the lesser in magnitude, though not in brightness, of the two which governed his destiny. 'Was it not', said Emma Hamilton to Nelson when she first greeted him after the battle of the Nile, 'the happiest day of your life?' 'No,' Nelson replied with unconscious irony, 'the happiest was the day I married Lady Nelson.'

Nelson has been much criticized for his conduct during the next eighteen months, which he spent mostly at Palermo in Sicily, whither he had conveyed the absurd King Ferdinand upon the approach of the French armies to Naples. Though much occupied with small business it was a time, on the whole, of inactivity, and it is evident that Nelson did not object to being inactive. It seems a little harsh to blame him. Emma Hamilton was undoubtedly one of the reasons which made him linger out the pleasant days; but there were others – his disappointment, for instance, at not being made Commander-in-Chief in the Mediterranean, and the plain fact that, at the moment, there was little to be done. One incident, however, was very unfortunate, and gave a convenient handle to Nelson's enemies: Lord Keith, who had succeeded St Vincent as Commander-in-Chief, had ordered Nelson to take command of the blockade of Malta. Nelson however pleaded ill-health and went back to Palermo. The moment after he left the squadron, the French ship *Guillaume Tell* – now the last survivor of de Brueys' fleet, for the only other ship of the line to escape had been destroyed shortly before by Nelson himself – slipped out of Valetta harbour and attempted to get away to France. She was caught and defeated, but – Nelson ought to have been there. A sick officer should apply for leave, and return to England. Nelson had not done so: he had returned not to England, but to Palermo. Shortly afterwards he received a tactfully-worded letter from the Admiralty: 'I believe', wrote Lord Spencer, 'that I am joined in opinion by all your friends here that you will be more likely to recover your health and strength in England than in any inactive situation in a foreign court, however pleasing the respect and gratitude shown to you for your services may be. . . . ' It was an order of recall, and Nelson could not ignore it. It so happened that at the same time Sir William Hamilton was superseded as

Ambassador at the court of Naples; so Nelson and the Hamiltons made the journey to England in company. Before he left, Nelson had been presented by King Ferdinand with the dukedom of Bronte.

The party travelled overland from Leghorn. It was a strange, though triumphal, progress, and 'Antony and his Moll Cleopatra' provided just the matter most suited to gossip-writers and evil tongues. All human truth, no doubt, is partial; it is as well, however, that the part should be not the least, but the most, significant that human wit can reach. Even the Roman Antony had qualities which redeemed the libertine. The three landed at Yarmouth. Burnham-Thorpe was only a few miles away; it was Nelson's own country, and the people took him to their hearts. Then they set out for London, where Lady Nelson was waiting to receive her husband.

It is a curious fact, and very revealing to anyone who wishes to understand Nelson's peculiar temperament, that he seems quite genuinely to have expected Lady Nelson to welcome the Hamiltons to her house. No man of the world could have been so innocent, or so ignorant – but one thinks of the poet Blake, who saw angels in the apple trees at Felpham, and was surprised rather than hurt when his wife objected to a rival, and of Shelley, who invited Harriett to live in amity with him and Mary Godwin. Nelson does not appear to have believed that his relationship with Emma Hamilton should in any way have affected his relationship with his wife. Lady Nelson, however, a woman by no means

> too bright or good
> For human nature's daily food,

thought otherwise. After a month or two of misery she and Nelson parted. Fanny Nelson outlived her husband twenty-six years; she is said to have talked of him to her friends with warmth and generosity to the end of her life, and to have done her best to palliate his conduct towards her.

Nelson was no sooner in England than he urged the Admiralty to appoint him to another command – a sufficient answer to the critics who supposed that Lady Hamilton's influence affected what always was, in spite of the months at Palermo, and continued to remain, the guiding passion of his life. In January 1801 he received orders to join St Vincent's fleet at Plymouth, and hoisted his flag in the *San Josef*. Just about the same time Lady Hamilton gave birth to a daughter, who was christened Horatia. The child was boarded out in London, and any chance he had (they were not many) in the next four years, he would take eagerly to visit her, and sit on the floor for hours, playing with her, as he had once played with Josiah in the Governor's house in Nevis. A few weeks later he shifted his flag to the *St George* and sailed to Yarmouth to join Admiral Sir Hyde Parker, who was bound for the Baltic on a difficult mission. Russia and the Scandinavian countries were neutral in the war, but hostile to Britain. Paul, the mad Tsar, desired Napoleon's friendship, and the other Scandinavian powers resented the right of search which was exercised by Britain as mistress of the sea. The result was the proclamation of 'armed neutrality', the refusal to recognize the right of search, and an embargo imposed by the Tsar upon British shipping in Russian ports. At the same time the French were putting pressure upon Denmark and Sweden to use their fleets against England. The situation was dangerous, and the British Government rightly felt that it was time to clarify it – the Scandinavian countries must either be the friends of England or her open enemies. Precisely what steps Admiral Parker was to take had been left to his judgement – or rather to his lack of it, for he was not a man to make bold decisions; fortunately, however, his second-in-command soon gained complete ascendancy at the council table, and poor Parker was pushed against his will into one of the most resounding naval victories of the war. 'A fleet of British ships of war', wrote Nelson, 'are the best negotiators in Europe.' Negotiation was, indeed, attempted, but the Danes firmly refused the British demands and the way was thus cleared for the use of force.

It was Nelson, not Parker, who drew up the plan for the attack upon the Danish fleet. His own preference was to go straight for the Russian fleet in Reval, but Parker could not be induced to risk so bold a move, and Nelson fell back upon his second alternative. Copenhagen was strongly defended: to the north was the powerful Trekroner battery, whose seventy guns protected the entrance to the harbour; southward from the battery was moored a line of eighteen dismasted battleships, heavily armed, along the narrow Inner, or King's, Channel, and four more in the actual harbour entrance. A mile-and-a-half stretch of shoal water, known as the Middle Ground, lay between the Inner and Outer channels. Nelson's plan, for which he got Parker's approval, was to take the twelve ships of the line which had the lightest draught, together with all the frigates, sail south down the Outer Channel and, as soon as the wind came fair, to round the shoal and enter the Inner Channel at its southern end. Parker, meanwhile, with the remainder of the fleet, was to demonstrate against the Trekroner battery to the northward. Like all Nelson's plans, it did the bold and unexpected thing – and succeeded, though not without heavy losses in men and gear, for the Danes proved themselves a courageous and determined enemy. The battle began badly for the British; for when the captains had been given their final instructions, the pilots (mostly merchant seamen accustomed to these waters) refused the responsibility of taking ships of the line into the narrow channel – all buoys had, of course, been removed by the Danes. At last the master of the *Bellona*, a Mr Briarly, one of the veterans of the Nile, volunteered to lead the column, and at 9.30 in the morning of 2 April 1801, the signal to weigh anchor in succession was hoisted. 'The *Edgar*', wrote Colonel Stewart in his account of the action, 'proceeded in a noble manner for the channel. Not a word was spoken through the ship save by the pilot and helmsman, and their commands, being chanted very much in the same manner as the responses in a cathedral service, added to the solemnity.' The *Edgar* got safely in, anchored, and opened fire; but the ship which should have followed her (Nelson's old *Agamemnon*) failed to clear the tail-end of the shoal and ran aground. Two others also grounded, so that Nelson's striking force was seriously reduced. The remainder, once they were in the channel, anchored by the stern, their sails still loose but clewed up to the yards, and the general action began. The frigates, under Captain Riou, held on to the northern end of the channel and engaged the Trekroner fort outside the entrance of the harbour. For some hours the fighting was violent and indecisive, the Danes continually replacing their crews as they fell by fresh men from the shore. Admiral Parker, on his station to the northward, and beating up against the southerly wind to get within range of the Trekroner fort, grew anxious as he watched through his glass the ding-dong struggle, and more and more convinced that Nelson would fail. At last he made the signal to discontinue the action. Nelson's signal officer asked if he should repeat the signal to the squadron. 'No,' answered Nelson, 'acknowledge it.' Meanwhile he was walking the quarter-deck rapidly and in evident agitation, waving the stump of his right arm – his 'fin'. Presently he turned to Colonel Stewart who was on deck beside him: 'Leave off action!' he exclaimed. 'Now damn me if I do.' Then to Captain Foley, his old friend, he added with a shrug of the shoulders, 'You know, Foley, I have only one eye. I have a right to be blind sometimes.' He put his glass to his blind eye, and announced: 'I really do not see the signal.' It was not the first time that Nelson had disobeyed an order. Riou, in command of the frigates, all of which had suffered severely from the guns of the Trekroner, drew off unwillingly. 'What will Nelson think of us?' he exclaimed – but was never to know, for at that instant, as his ship presented her stern to the fort, a round-shot killed him.

By two o'clock in the afternoon the Danish fire had almost ceased, but kept breaking out again as fresh parties from the shore came aboard ships which had already struck. Nelson sent a note to the Danish Crown Prince, in which he threatened that, unless all firing stopped at once, he would burn every prize he had taken, crews and all. It was a savage threat, but it had its effect, and saved many lives both Danish and British. An armistice was agreed upon, and Nelson went ashore to conduct negotiations in person. As he passed through the streets of Copenhagen, the crowds cheered him. Soon after the battle the Tsar was assassinated, and the threat to England from the north was finally removed.

Nelson, now made a viscount, remained in the Baltic for a further three months – in command, for Admiral Parker had been recalled. As usual after a great action, he was depressed, nervous, and ill; and he hated the chilly north. But some of the pleasantest stories about him refer to this time, especially, perhaps, the story of how he would invite his midshipmen, tired after a night watch, to breakfast with him at five o'clock in the morning, to share their jokes and talk familiarly of what interested or amused them.

Back in England soon after midsummer, he was welcomed, as always, by the people with extravagant love; but he was not happy. He was still a sick man, and the perfectly natural refusal of society to recognize Lady Hamilton filled him with resentment. He was irritable and restless and, contrary to his usual custom, shrank from the expression of public devotion which he had inspired. 'Oh, how I hate to be stared at!' he wrote, and had the door fiercely shut against strangers who hoped for a sight of him – as if he were to be 'shown about like a beast'. The long years of strain were telling on him, and his nerves were on edge. He asked Lady Hamilton to find a house in the country, where they might live if peace should come, as he hoped it would. But what came was only half a peace: war ceased, by the treaty of Lunéville, on the continent of Europe, but England continued to hold out against Napoleon, who now began to mass an army at Boulogne in the attempt to scare his obstinate enemy by the threat of invasion. They were anxious days. The admiral in the Downs was Lutwidge, Nelson's old friend and a fine officer well capable of dealing with any attempt the French might make to cross the Channel; but what the British Government wanted was a name of power to set against the goblin name of 'Boney'; and that name was obviously Nelson's. He was asked accordingly to take command of all frigates and small craft for defence of the coast between Orfordness and Beachy Head. He accepted without hesitation, and, less than a month after his return from the Baltic, hoisted his flag in the frigate *Medusa*. What is most memorable, perhaps, in this brief period of minor service, is not the unsuccessful cutting-out expedition against Boulogne, but Nelson's grief at the death of a young and obscure junior officer called Edward Parker. Nelson had met Parker in the Baltic, and had taken to him at once, as he had taken to many another promising young man, and generously befriended him. During the boat-attack in Boulogne harbour Parker was shot through the thigh. He was put into hospital at Deal, and Nelson would visit him whenever he could, and spend hours by his bed, promising, when he should recover, to take him to his 'Farm' (as he called the house at Merton, which had now become his property) to regain his strength. But the boy – he was little more – died. Nelson was inconsolable: 'He was my child,' he wrote, 'for I found him in distress.' At the funeral he wept. 'Thank God,' he wrote, 'the dreadful scene is past. I could not suffer much more and be alive.' Perhaps the most remarkable power which the human mind possesses is the power to irradiate and transform; without it, a man as easily moved as Nelson was to love and pity, could hardly have endured a lifetime of familiar companionship with the brutality of war.

In October the Peace of Amiens was concluded. Nelson was kept at sea a few weeks longer, tossing in his frigate in the autumn gales, in worse health than ever, and dreadfully seasick. At last, towards the end of the month, his release came and he hurried to Merton – the only home he had ever had since his boyhood days.

But it was only a poor shadow of peace; nobody in England who was in touch with affairs, least of all Nelson himself, ever expected that Napoleon would use it for any purpose other than that of strengthening his position on the Continent, and it was clear that the war must sooner or later be renewed. Meanwhile Nelson had his brief respite at Merton. A nephew of his remembered him at that time as 'dressed always in a plain suit of black', a small, quiet, unobtrusive figure, talking little, and never, if he could avoid it, of his own exploits. He liked to dispense charity to the villagers, and regularly attended church. In the spring of 1803 Sir William Hamilton died, and Nelson and Lady Hamilton were able to live as man and wife, and little Horatia was sent for from London to join them. But they had no more than a single month; for in May war was declared again, and Nelson was needed to serve – and to save – his country. Four days after the declaration of war he sailed from Portsmouth in the *Victory* to join the Mediterranean fleet as Commander-in-Chief.

Napoleon wished the war to be renewed, and had, indeed, done everything in his power to make a renewal of it inevitable; nevertheless, he was not ready for it when it came. In particular, he was short of ships; a number were building, but not yet ready for sea, and his available fleets were incapable of meeting the British on favourable terms. When war started, they were all concentrated in the three great harbours of Brest, Cadiz, and Toulon, and it was the business of the British fleets to keep them there, or, if they ventured out, to catch and destroy them. Napoleon was still planning to invade England; he had sufficient troops in readiness on the Channel coast, but they could not cross without a fleet to protect them; it was therefore of vital importance that no French fleet should be allowed to get into the Channel. Brest was blockaded by Cornwallis, Cadiz by Collingwood, and Nelson's task was to watch the mouth of the Adriatic, the Straits of Messina and, in particular, Toulon. It was the beginning of his most arduous, but least spectacular, service. War a hundred and fifty years ago was not like war today; the comfortable classes in England continued to live as comfortably as ever, and few amongst them, one guesses, were vividly aware of that silent and unceasing watch, that relentless stranglehold upon the Atlantic and Mediterranean coasts of France, continuing month after month, year after year, in all seasons and all weathers; which in fact contributed as much as anything else to the final defeat of Napoleon. For eighteen months not a single French ship got out of Toulon harbour; for two whole years Nelson was aboard the *Victory* without once setting foot ashore. It was a test of endurance both for ships and crews unparalleled in the history of the war, and, simply as such, a remarkable achievement; but what is more interesting is the light it throws upon an aspect of Nelson which, in one's preoccupation with him as an inspired fighter, it is easy to overlook – his sheer *competence* as a commander. That Nelson was loved, everybody knows; but mere devotion to a commander is not enough to keep men eager and alert for a two-year spell at sea, during which nothing of importance occurred. That Nelson succeeded in keeping his crews both happy and efficient is attested by every contemporary authority. He gave them continually as much change of occupation and scene as he could, and organized entertainments for them on board; above all, he kept them healthy – often the *Victory*, with her crew of 840 men, had not a single one on the sick list – for those days (and indeed for any days) an astonishing achievement. Ever since 1782 when, in the *Albemarle*, he had had experience of scurvy, Nelson had paid careful attention to the seamen's diet, and his service in this vital matter was perhaps surpassed only by that of the great navigator James Cook. Throughout the blockade his men were never without fresh vegetables, especially onions, in the virtue of which he was a firm believer. His own health, also, was comparatively good. 'We are in great good humour with ourselves,' he wrote, 'and so sharp set that I would not be a French Admiral in the way of some of our ships for something. I believe we are in the right fighting trim: let them come as soon as they please.' A pleasant picture of life in the *Victory* at this time has been left by one of her surgeons: breakfast of 'tea, toast, hot rolls, cold tongue, etc.' would be served soon after six in the Admiral's cabin, where Hardy (in command of the ship), Rear-Admiral Murray, the Captain of the Fleet, Nelson's chaplain Dr Scott and his secretary John Scott, and one or two other officers would be assembled;

routine business would occupy the rest of the morning, and at two o'clock a string-band would play for an hour until dinner, the chief meal of the day, occupying an hour and a half or two hours. Nelson himself ate little, and drank less, but during these long sessions at the dinner table he seems to have been at his best and happiest: hospitable, easy in manner, and attentive to everyone. By nine o'clock he was generally in bed, but not for long; he seldom slept for more than two hours on end, spending much time, when no particular business called, walking the quarterdeck, day or night, usually ill-clad against cold or wet, and invariably wearing thin shoes, or pumps, which he would kick off on returning to his cabin, and walk the carpet until his stockings dried. He enjoyed chaffing Dr Scott (who adored him) over the after-dinner wine, leading him on to dispute with Captain Hardy upon some question of seamanship well beyond his province: 'Ah, my dear doctor,' he would say, 'give me knowledge *practically* acquired.' It was Dr Scott ('at times wrong in the head; absolutely too much learning has turned him', wrote Nelson to Emma) who sat weeping night after night by Nelson's body on its last voyage home after Trafalgar. 'I never knew', he said, 'how much I loved him. I become stupid with grief for what I have lost.'

And so the blockade went on until the January of 1805; then, when the fleet was in the Sardinian port of Maddalena, taking in water, a frigate was seen approaching with the long-awaited signal that the French were at sea. Villeneuve had slipped out of Toulon the previous night, and had been last seen off Corsica, sailing south. Where was he bound? It was the old game again. The wind was strong from the north-west, so he could not be making for Gibraltar and the Atlantic. Nelson laid his course for Egypt. The French were not there, so he returned – and found them back in Toulon. Three weeks later, as the *Victory* was on her way to her station west of Toulon, Nelson learnt that they were out again; this time the wind was easterly, and Villeneuve had made the most of it to get through the Straits. This, however, Nelson did not yet know, and he had to make sure that the Frenchmen's destination was not the East before he could dare to leave the Mediterranean. Thus he started on his long chase a full month behind his enemy. Villeneuve's orders were to go to the West Indies and, after doing what damage he could to British commerce and possessions, to link up with the Brest fleet, if it should succeed in slipping through the block-ade, and then, with the combined fleets, to get temporary control of the English Channel. Nelson's object was to catch Villeneuve, destroy his fleet, and prevent the junction. Neither succeeded; the Brest fleet did not get out, and Nelson, by a series of accidents, failed to find Villeneuve amongst the islands. Early in June Ville-neuve sailed again for Europe, and five days later Nelson was after him. He landed in Gibraltar on July 20th – the first time he had been ashore since June two years pre-viously. Villeneuve, arriving off Rochefort, fell in with a British squadron under Sir Robert Calder, in thick weather, and an indecisive engagement took place. He then, with the loss of two ships, put into Vigo. A few days later Napoleon was at Boulogne, reviewing the troops intended for the invasion of England – if ever the sails of Villeneuve's ships should appear in the Channel. But they never did.

Nelson, before he left the Mediterranean on his Atlantic chase, had received a letter from the Admiralty authorizing him to return to England on sick leave. Now at last he made use of it; he sailed to Spithead, landed, and hurried home to Merton where Emma was waiting for him. He was well aware that the respite would be brief. Much of his time was occupied by interviews in

London with ministers, and all too soon it was reported that the French were out again. Calder was after them, and for some days Nelson hoped for news of a successful engagement. None came, and Nelson knew with growing certainty that he would be needed very soon. He called on Pitt, and put to him his belief that the combined fleets of France and Spain were making not, as the cabinet thought, for the West Indies, but for Cadiz; and the two men agreed upon the number of British ships which would be needed to attack them. 'Now,' said Pitt, 'who is to take command?' 'You cannot', replied Nelson, 'have a better man than the present one – Collingwood.' 'That won't do,' said Pitt; '*you* must take command' – and asked him to be ready in three days. 'I am ready now,' was Nelson's answer. At five o'clock next morning Captain Blackwood, on his way to London with dispatches from Collingwood, called at Merton. Nelson was already dressed. 'You bring news', he said, 'of the French and Spanish fleets. I shall have to beat them yet.' It was true; the enemy, as Nelson had already guessed, were in Cadiz. On the evening of September 13th he left Merton in a post-chaise for Portsmouth. Emma bade him a most brave farewell. Before he left, he went to the bedroom of little Horatia, now five years old. She was asleep, and he knelt by her bed and prayed that her life might be a happy one. Later the same night he wrote in his diary: 'Drove from dear, dear Merton, where I left all which I hold dear in this world. . . . May the great God whom I adore enable me to fulfil the expectations of my country. If it is His good Providence to cut short my days upon earth, I bow with the greatest submission, relying that He will protect those so dear to me, that I may leave behind. His will be done. Amen. Amen. Amen.' Ever since he came ashore on August 19th, the presentiment of death had been growing on him; it was shortly to become an absolute assurance. No man ever knew with greater certainty that his time was short, and his work soon to be accomplished.

The *Victory* was lying in St Helen's roads, and on the following day Nelson was aboard. He had ordered the boat to take him off from the beach at Southsea, hoping to avoid a crowd. He did not succeed: people packed the by-lanes and back-streets to see him pass, falling to their knees and weeping. On the beach itself they swarmed into the water as the boat pushed off. 'I had their huzzas before,' he said to Hardy; 'I have now their hearts.' The *Victory* weighed anchor without delay; after a slow passage with foul winds down Channel, she joined Collingwood's fleet off Cadiz on September 28th, and Nelson took over the command. He had sent a frigate in advance with orders that no salute should be fired on his arrival, which he wished to conceal from Villeneuve. Throughout the British fleet his coming brought, as one captain put it, 'a sort of general joy'. 'The reception I met with on joining the fleet', said Nelson, 'caused the sweetest sensation of my life. The officers who came on board to welcome my return forgot my rank as commander-in-chief, in the enthusiasm with which they greeted me.' He laid before them his plan of attack. 'Some wept,' says Nelson of these hardened veterans of many fights; 'all approved.' It was the strangest scene, and yet – not strange; for Nelson had a power over men which inspired something beyond confidence and courage.

Villeneuve's ships were lying in the outer harbour of Cadiz, watched closely by the British frigates; Nelson's ships of the line were fifty miles out in the Atlantic, awaiting the signal. Villeneuve, though Nelson did not know it, had already had orders from Napoleon to make for Toulon, whether or not the British should be in the way, and had been threatened with dismissal if he failed. All he needed was a fair wind, to get him clear of Cadiz.

On the 19th of October the wind came easterly. It was Villeneuve's chance, and at daylight the combined fleet began to move. By 9.30 in the morning the British frigates had seen them, and the signal, from masthead to masthead, was passed to the *Victory*, fifty miles away. Next morning the wind went into the sou'-west and the French were getting an offing before turning southwards for Gibraltar; Nelson, now sure of their intention, laid his course directly for the Strait. At dawn on the 21st, the wind having veered nor'-west, the two fleets were in sight of one another. The *Victory*'s signal officer, going to Nelson's cabin for instructions, found him on his knees, writing: 'May the Great God, whom I worship, grant to my country a great and glorious victory; and may no misconduct in anyone tarnish it; and may humanity after victory be the predominant feature in the British fleet. For myself, I commit my life to Him who made it. . . . To Him I resign myself and the just Cause which is entrusted to me to defend. Amen, Amen, Amen.' Then he called for Hardy to witness the codicil to his will, by which he left Lady Hamilton as 'a legacy to my King and Country, that they will give her an ample provision to maintain her rank in life'. For his daughter Horatia he asked the same, adding: 'these are the only favours I ask of my King and Country at this moment when I am going to fight their battle'. He was quite certain that the coming battle would be his last.

Villeneuve had thirty-three ships to Nelson's twenty-seven, but even now he hoped to avoid a general action, and altered course for Cadiz again. The British were drawing towards his line at right angles in two columns, about a mile apart, that to the southward led by Collingwood in the *Royal Sovereign*, the other, to the northward, by Nelson in the *Victory*. The wind was very light and there was a long swell, the forerunner of a gale. Slowly the three lines converged. Nelson had intended to repeat the tactics of St Vincent, cutting off and enveloping the rear portion of the French line and destroying it before the leading ships could come to its assistance; but now, in the poor wind, this could not be done, and the only way to prevent Villeneuve from getting most of his fleet back into Cadiz was to hold directly on as he was going. This meant that the leading ships of the two British columns, his own and Collingwood's, would have to approach the French line bows-on, and so be raked, with the certainty of heavy casualties. Blackwood, who was with Nelson on the quarterdeck, begged him to allow the two ships next astern to go ahead. 'Very well,' answered Nelson, 'let them – if they can.' One of them, the *Temeraire*, made up on the *Victory*, and drew level; but, as she ranged alongside, Nelson hailed her: 'I'll thank you, Captain Harvey, to keep in your proper station, which is astern of the *Victory*.' Then he said to Blackwood: 'I'll give them such a dressing as they never had before.' The French line was now very near. It was time for Blackwood to return to his frigate; as he went down the side into his boat he wished his commander good luck and said good-bye. 'God bless you Blackwood,' was Nelson's answer; 'I shall never speak to you again.'

A few minutes before, standing on the poop, he had announced his intention of 'amusing the fleet a little', and the famous signal ENGLAND EXPECTS THAT EVERY MAN WILL DO HIS DUTY had fluttered to the masthead.

The *Royal Sovereign*, to leeward, was the first to reach the French line. Coming under a tremendous raking fire, which killed or wounded nearly six hundred of her men, she rounded up close under the stern of the Spanish *Santa Ana*. Nelson was watching her through his glass. 'See', he exclaimed, 'how that noble fellow Collingwood carries his ship into action!' Meanwhile the *Victory*, creeping forward over the long smooth swells with every stitch of canvas set, had come under fire from the centre of the enemy line. Fifty of her men were killed, but she made, as yet, no reply. Her mizzen-topmast was shot away; Nelson's secretary, Scott, was killed beside him on the poop. Then her wheel was smashed, and she had to be steered by the tiller, with heavy tackles, from the lower gun-deck. Still she reserved her fire until, just before one o'clock in the afternoon, she crawled up under the stern of the *Bucentaure*, Villeneuve's flagship, so close that the two ships actually touched. Then, as the *Victory* slid past each gun as it bore raked the enemy clear along her length from stern to bows. Behind the *Bucentaure* were two other French ships, *Redoutable* and *Neptune*, so close that there was not room for the *Victory* to pass clear. Hardy informed Nelson that it was impossible to cut the line without falling foul of one or the other of them, and Nelson answered, 'I can't help it; it does not signify which you run on board of. Take your choice.' Hardy chose the *Redoutable*. There was a crash as the two ships collided, and one of the *Victory*'s yard-arms hung up in her enemy's rigging. They were locked together. At the range of a few feet the *Victory*'s starboard broadside poured into the *Redoutable*, her port guns blazing at the *Santissima Trinidad*, lying just ahead of Villeneuve. The *Redoutable* closed her gun-ports, and a boarding-party made ready, while men, crowded in her tops, attempted to clear the *Victory*'s upper deck with hand-grenades and musket fire. The two ships were rolling heavily in the swell making accurate aim difficult. Nelson and Hardy, side by side, were walking the quarterdeck – back and forth, back and forth. Suddenly Hardy realized that he was alone; he turned, and saw Nelson on his knees, his one hand pressing the deck. Then the arm gave way and he fell on his side. Hardy bent over him. Nelson smiled; 'Hardy,' he said, 'I believe they have done for me at last.' A musket-ball had entered his left shoulder from above, and broken his backbone. He was carried below to the cockpit, already filled with dead or desperately wounded men 'like a butcher's shambles' as poor Dr Scott shudderingly described it – and laid in the midshipmen's berth. As they lifted him, he had covered his face with a handkerchief, that men might not recognize him and lose heart. He lived for three hours, in great pain, Dr Scott by his side, bewildered with grief. Hardy, when he could leave the deck, came to him with news that the battle was won, with fourteen or fifteen French ships taken. Later he came again, and took Nelson's hand, unable to speak. Another broadside roared. 'O *Victory*, *Victory*,' muttered Nelson, 'how you distract my poor brain!' Then he added, 'How dear is life to all men!' Turning his eyes to Hardy, 'I hope', he said, 'none of *our* ships have struck?' 'No, my lord,' was the answer; 'there is no fear of that.' Emma Hamilton was vivid in his now darkening brain – Dr Scott was to let her have his hair. 'Doctor,' he said, 'I have not been a *great* sinner.' Hardy, at the Admiral's request, knelt and kissed his cheek, stood for a minute speechless, then knelt again and kissed his forehead. 'Who is that?' whispered Nelson. 'It is Hardy.' 'God bless you, Hardy,' was the answer. Almost his last words were to urge Hardy to anchor, to save the half-crippled and unhandy ships from driving ashore in the sou'-westerly gale which he knew was on the way. As his speech failed, he was heard to mutter, 'Thank God – I have done my duty'. An orderly, watching, went and whispered something to Beatty, the chief surgeon, who was busy with others, and Beatty, as he had done at frequent intervals during the past hour, hurried again to Nelson's side. He was dead; and Dr Scott was still mechanically chafing his breast.

Trafalgar was the most complete of all British naval victories, but it is hard to say whether the news of it brought to England greater sorrow or relief. Nelson's body was brought home in the *Victory* – he had himself asked Hardy not to 'throw him overboard'. He was buried in St Paul's on 9 January 1806. The immense crowds which lined the streets as the long procession passed were silent, the only sound, caused by the movement to uncover as the funeral car came into sight, being like a 'murmur of the sea'. Twelve seamen from the *Victory* carried the coffin from the car.

Nelson's brother, who succeeded him in the viscounty, was made an earl. A grateful country did not, however, accept the legacy of Emma Hamilton. Nelson himself had left her well enough off, but she ran into debt and died poor and forgotten in Calais, nine years later.

One small anecdote must be added, for it enables us, perhaps better than any other, to see why it was that Nelson reigned so royally in the hearts of his 'poor brave fellows'. Before Trafalgar, he happened to discover that a coxswain had been so busy preparing the mailbags on board the *Victory* that he forgot to put into them his own letter to his wife, and remembered the omission only after the dispatch vessel had sailed. 'Hoist a signal to bring her back,' said Nelson. 'Who knows but that he may fall in action tomorrow? His letter shall go with the rest.' The signal was made, and, for the sake of that one letter, the dispatch ship was recalled.

Sir Francis Drake. Artist Unknown.
Reproduced by kind permission of the National Portrait Gallery

Viscount Nelson. From a painting by
L. F. Abbott. *Reproduced by kind permission
of the National Portrait Gallery*

Dr Samuel Johnson. From a portrait by
J. Barry. *Reproduced by kind permission
of the National Portrait Gallery*

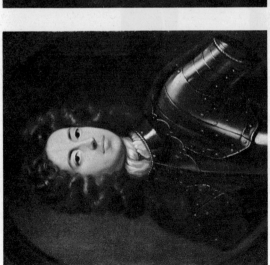

The Duke of Marlborough.
From a painting by John Closterman.
*Reproduced by kind permission of the
National Portrait Gallery*

John Keats.
By W. Hilton after a miniature by J. Severn.
*Reproduced by kind permission of the
National Portrait Gallery*

Sir Winston Churchill at Southampton Civic Centre, January 1941. *Reproduced by kind permission of the Imperial War Museum*

Marlborough

MORE people read novels than histories or biographies, and a good novelist who introduces historical characters into his story has immense influence, both through the magic of his art and the number of his readers, in fixing the popular conception of what those characters were like. How many people, for instance, have assumed that the amiable and excellent Leigh Hunt was no better than Skimpole in Dickens's *Bleak House*? And how many people have been content to form their picture of John Churchill, first Duke of Marlborough, according to the brutal travesty in Thackeray's *Esmond* – especially if they have chanced to pass from *Esmond* to a reading of Macaulay, who ought to have known better?

It is worth considering, at the outset, two reasons why Marlborough, whom even his enemies recognized as the finest soldier, and perhaps the ablest statesman, of his age, should have been subjected for so long to calumny in his character as a man. The first springs from the nature of the times in which Marlborough lived. During the latter half of the seventeenth century, and until the accession of George I in 1714, England was in labour to produce the infant constitution which has since grown into what we know today. Cromwell had by no means made an end of the civil war, though he had put a stop to the fighting; the war continued, bloodless indeed, except for the brief episode of Monmouth's rebellion, but violent, passionate, and continually on the verge of blood. The life of peasant and artisan in village, farm, and workshop continued much as it had been for centuries – tough, durable, and dumb – and as it was still to continue for more than another hundred years, excluded from any share in public affairs and occupied solely in the primary interests of work, food, and worship; but the governing class, a comparatively small group of a few thousand families – consisting for the most part of able men, more or less intimately known to one another – was split into opposing factions, each of which fought the other partly for personal ascendancy (for at that time, unlike the present day, political office carried with it the opportunity of splendid rewards), and partly for the realization of its own vision of what England should be, with an intensity never seen before or since in our history. More than ever, in those days, politics (the art of living together) and religion (the making of one's peace with God) were the causes of setting men at one another's throats, and they joined battle with a zest and fury not easy to understand in these milder times. We, having grown polite, reserve our major lies and calumnies for international disputes; but not so the men of Marlborough's age, when no weapon was too sordid or too mean to blacken the character or ruin the credit of a political opponent. Now when it is realized that the Duke of Marlborough, shunning what he called 'the detested names of Whig and Tory', refused throughout his long career to give his whole-hearted allegiance to either, and consequently incurred at various times the enmity of both, it is not hard to understand why he was seldom free from obloquy; and when it is further realized that, in the latter part of his life, when the furtherance of his grand design brought him into conjunction with the Whigs, the Tories hired not only the most brilliant writers of the day, like Swift, but also the most scurrilous, like Mrs Manley, to vilify him, it is easy to see how subsequent generations began to build up their picture of his character.

The second reason is a subtler one. Marlborough

appears in history almost entirely as a public character; about his private and personal life – apart from one cardinal fact, the forty-five years of single-hearted devotion to his wife – very little is known. The reason for this blank in our knowledge is not far to seek – James Boswell had not yet been born; and before the appearance in 1791 of Boswell's *Life of Johnson*, that great book which changed the nature of biography, the little revealing intimacies of a man's life, his tone of voice, his manner of sitting at table, and what he took for his tea, were considered to be beneath the notice of public attention. This, combined with the fact that Marlborough seems to have had little or nothing of that quality which appeals, as in men like Nelson, to the romantic sentiment of ordinary people, has inevitably told against him. The better we know our heroes, the better we love them. We admire achievement, but we love a man. Those who are chilled by the self-advertisement of Byron, his treatment of women, and his vulgar abuse of Keats, are insensibly drawn to him when they are given a glimpse into the more secret places of that flamboyant character, and see it melt into admiration and tenderness under Shelley's spell – or read the story of how he grew so fond of the geese he was fattening for a Christmas dinner that he could not bring himself to kill them. But in Marlborough these secret places of the heart are almost wholly closed to us, and we have little more to set against the glittering tale of his long campaigns and relentless political struggle than we have in Pericles or Caesar. As a man, Marlborough tends to elude us, unless we are willing to take the word of his many detractors who, in their turn, drew his picture from materials richly supplied by his political enemies, who hated him in exact proportion to his power and success. 'He loved lucre', Macaulay has told us, 'more than wine or women'; perhaps he did – it may well be that drunkenness or profligacy were less important to him than thrift and the founding of a fortune; yet Macaulay's ambiguous but famous phrase ignores the fact that Marlborough's wife was a woman, and that he rejected a wealthy heiress in order to marry her with hardly a penny in his pocket, and continued to love her until he died.

Five times in modern history the independence of England has been threatened by the rise of a foreign power and its attempt at European, or world, dominion: once by Spain, twice by France, and twice, in our own day, by Germany. History is more than the lives and exploits of individuals; yet though the blind but potent forces which work out their purpose through the mass of a race or people have more power to shape its destiny than any single man, it is none the less hard for our partial and personalizing eye not to see, at each crisis, those complex forces focused, as it were, and centred in the dominating figure of a single leader, who seems to control the very circumstances which produced him. Such a figure was Drake; such were Chatham and Nelson and Wellington and Winston Churchill; and such, as even his enemies admitted, was the Duke of Marlborough, who more than any other one man of his epoch was responsible for saving England from becoming a dependency of France, and as much as any for the two necessary adjuncts to that supreme task, the securing of the Protestant succession to the English throne and the establishment on a firm basis of the Constitutional Monarchy, upon which the subsequent political greatness of Britain has been built.

John Churchill, the eldest surviving son of Winston Churchill, was born at his grandmother's home, Ashe House, between Lyme Regis and Axminster in Devon, on 24 May 1650. He was one of eleven children, of whom four grew up. The stresses of the household at Ashe must have been typical of those in many other homes during the harsh days of civil war; for John's grandmother, Lady Drake, was the widow of Sir John Drake who had fought for the Parliament, and John's father, Winston, had, as a young man, become a passionate supporter of the Royalists. Moreover, the family was in great straits for money. Children matured more quickly then than they do nowadays, and by the time John Churchill went to St Paul's school at the age of eleven, he must already have received strong impressions both of the bitterness of poverty and of the merciless nature of political strife, which helped to form his attitude to the difficult and dangerous world into which he had been born: a world in which religion was taken very seriously, while, at the same time, Christian principles were found to be singularly inapplicable to public, and singularly inconvenient to private, affairs, and the conflict of loyalties often made it necessary for the best men to abandon a friend in the interest of party or nation, and still oftener, perhaps, induced the worst to abandon all ties whatever in the interest of personal ambition.

Meanwhile, however, John's father, Sir Winston, shortly after the Restoration, had been established at Court as a reward for his services in the Royalist cause, and was consequently able to do something for his son's advancement. The eldest child of the family, Arabella, had already been appointed to the position of maid of honour to the Duchess of York, and a year later John, now sixteen, was made page to the Duke – the King's brother and afterwards King James II. It was his first step on the road to fame. In Stuart England careers were not open to talent alone; promotion was by favour and patronage, and John knew well enough that luck for the first time had come his way. He was young, good-looking, capable, and ambitious, and now he had a noble master who might put him in the way of advancement. From the moment he entered the Duke's service, he was determined to be a match for the world and to put behind him for ever the narrow and ignominious life of obscure poverty in which he had passed his early years.

It was the Duke of York's practice frequently to review the Guards in Hyde Park, and on some occasions his page would accompany him. The story goes that once the Duke, observing the boy's interest in the ceremony, asked him what profession he would best like to enter. 'Give me', said John, falling upon his knees, 'a pair of colours in one of these fine regiments.' The request was granted, and, at the age of seventeen, John Churchill's military career had begun.

About the same time he met at Court Barbara Villiers, afterwards Duchess of Cleveland, his second cousin and the mistress for many years of Charles II. She was nine years his senior, beautiful, capricious, and passionate. The two at once became friends, and, a few years later, after Churchill's return from service in Tangier in 1671, lovers. Churchill was still poor; Barbara was rich. She gave him £5,000, with which he bought an annuity of £500 for life, and thus secured an independence. He was a provident young man. About the same time as his first meeting with the Duchess of Cleveland he made the acquaintance at Court of Sidney Godolphin, a man five years older than himself. The two were at once drawn together, and a life-long friendship began of great moment to the future history of England. It was to be cemented later by the marriage of Godolphin's son to one of Marlborough's daughters, and it was not to be broken by misfortune. Marlborough was lucky in his friendships – if, indeed, luck has anything to do with such things; no less remarkable than his long political association with Godolphin was his military association, in later years, with Prince Eugene of Savoy: the two men, peers in the realm of war, were to be bound together by affection and mutual respect, unmarred by the least touch of jealousy, to the inestimable benefit of England. This, together with his marriage, is worth remembering of the man who, Thackeray tells us, was incapable of love.

By one of the curious shifts of Charles II's foreign policy, Marlborough learned his first serious lessons in the art of war from the generals of the nation of whose defeat he was later to prove the chief architect. The Triple Alliance of England, Holland, and Sweden, negotiated in 1668 by Sir William Temple to check the advance of the French along the Rhine and into the Spanish Netherlands, was suddenly dissolved two years later. Charles, doubtful, perhaps, of the Dutch, and certain of his inability to oppose France unaided, concluded with Louis XIV the notorious Treaty of Dover. By the terms of this treaty, France with the help of England was to attack and partition Holland, the only European state to have offered effective resistance to French expansion hitherto, and England, in exchange, was to receive certain safeguards for her naval requirements and colonial ambitions. Secret clauses in the treaty further provided that Louis should furnish Charles with money and troops in England, in order that he might be strong enough to proclaim himself a Catholic and begin the task of raising fellow Catholics to a dominant position in the country.

Thus it happened that John Churchill found himself in the year 1672 a Captain of Grenadiers under the Duke of Monmouth in the army commanded by the two French marshals Turenne and the Prince de Condé. The young officer (Turenne called him 'my handsome Englishman') at once distinguished himself by his dash and daring, and in two years' time was promoted to the rank of Colonel. What he thought of the political implications of this campaign is not recorded; perhaps he considered it merely as valuable experience in his chosen profession of arms. That it certainly was, and Marshal Turenne little thought that he was helping to train in his handsome Englishman the most formidable enemy his country had ever known.

In the intervals of campaigning (it was the agreeable custom of those days for the troops to be withdrawn into winter quarters, as the season advanced and the weather became too unpleasant for fighting), Churchill returned to his duties at the Court of the King's brother, where he was soon made a Gentleman of the Wardrobe and admitted to the close confidence of his master. In 1673 Sarah Jennings, the twelve-year-old daughter of a Somersetshire squire, became attached to the household of the Duke of York. She was a brilliant and lively child, with good looks, a violent temper, and an unappeasable appetite for life. From her first coming into the Court, she and John Churchill must constantly have met, and three years later they fell in love. Barbara – if indeed she still had any place in Churchill's heart – was forgotten at once and for ever. For the remainder of his life he had no eyes for any woman but Sarah, nor she for any other man.

Churchill was still poor, and his parents were naturally opposed to the marriage. He had to live, and there were no immediate prospects of advancement. The connexion between love and marriage was by no means so close then as it is supposed to be today; it was still an age of *mariages de convenance*. A rich heiress, Catharine Sedley, was produced for John's approval. Would he not be sensible, and take her? He would only be doing what ninety-nine out of a hundred other young men would do as a matter of course under similar circumstances. Custom is a potent master, a spirit 'ill to guide but mighty to obey'. Churchill was ambitious; he hated poverty. For a while he hesitated; the courtship of Sarah dragged on into its second year, and then he yielded to what was, in a true sense, his destiny. Some time in the winter of 1677–8 he and Sarah were married. He was twenty-seven, and Sarah was seventeen.

Circumstances made the first few years of the Churchills' married life far from tranquil. In the close confidence of the Duke of York, Churchill was now increasingly employed upon diplomatic service when he was not actively engaged in the field. Again the European scene had shifted; the threat by France of becoming mistress of Belgium and the Channel ports raised the age-old recurring issue upon which England has so often been compelled to fight for her life. It was the issue of 1588 – the Armada year – of 1793, of 1914, and of 1939. The prospect or the presence of powerful hostile fleets and armies at the mouth of the Scheldt has always been a nightmare menace to England. The King was obliged by the strength of feeling in the country to abandon his Roman Catholic schemes, to make friends with the Dutch again, and endeavour to stave off, if he could, open war with France. Holland was saved, and tentative beginnings were made to found for resistance to France the confederacy of European states which, with England as paymaster, the Duke of Marlborough was to lead to victory during the reign of Queen Anne. Then, in 1677, by the marriage of Mary, daughter of the Duke of York, and heir, after her father, to the English throne, to William of Orange another spanner was flung into the machinery of Charles's intrigues with Catholic France. Churchill was employed upon a number of delicate diplomatic missions abroad; he was sent to Holland in 1678, with the authority of the King to arrange with the Dutch and the Spaniards the strength of the military and naval forces to be maintained by the new alliance against France, and frequently during the periods of the Duke's enforced sojourns either at The Hague or Brussels or in Scotland, Churchill, as his trusted agent, acted for him at the English Court or in France. In the meanwhile, moreover, he had been appointed Brigadier of Foot with the British troops in Flanders. Thus his career of combined diplomacy and arms, to be followed so brilliantly during his great period nearly a quarter of a century later in the reign of Anne, had already begun. Character and circumstance both fitted him for the task: he was the subtlest and most discreet of men, and the fact that he was a staunch and declared Protestant, an undeviating enemy to Louis XIV's ambition for world dominion, and at the time the most intimate and trusted servant of the Catholic heir to the English throne, enabled him to make connexions in every camp and to gather an unrivalled knowledge of the complex political scene. For his services during this period he was created Baron Churchill, of Aymouth, in Scotland, and in 1683 was made Colonel of the Royal Regiment of Horse Guards then about to be raised.

It is a fact to be remembered that throughout his long life Marlborough never wholly broke off his relations with the exiled Court and the Jacobites; he continued after the Revolution to correspond with James II at the Court of St Germain – despite his desertion of him in the field when William of Orange landed at Brixham. This refusal by Marlborough to sever all ties with the exiled Court of St Germain has of course been used against him as evidence of double-dealing, just as he has been accused of treachery for his desertion of James. The charge is easy to make and difficult to refute; perhaps it cannot be wholly refuted; it is worth, however, bearing in mind that politics in all ages has had scant respect for persons and is seldom subject to the code of conduct which regulates the easy intimacy of friends, and that in the period which preceded the Revolution of 1688 the excessive violence and confusion of political strife, aggravated by the religious issues involved, together with the dreadful uncertainties which the future held, were bound to lead even the best of men to 'take a bond of fate' and to seek some assurance that, if the worst happened, they might still have some chance of serving, or of saving, the political principles which they held dear. Marlborough was amongst the most active in bringing over the Prince of Orange; yet, until the actual landing of the Prince in England, he continued to allow James to believe that he was to be trusted in his cause. Not till he was made Lieutenant-General of the royal forces did he actually desert to the invader. The deed looks black enough, and only the temper of the times can excuse it. Churchill had to make a cruel choice; he had to choose between the betrayal of a benefactor and the worse betrayal of all he had worked for, and was to continue to work for until his death – a Protestant England under a limited monarchy, free from the dominion of France. It was hard, but one cannot believe that he hesitated; the moment of his desertion of James was ruthlessly and skilfully chosen: it was the moment when it would have most effect. Long before the crisis he had made perfectly clear to James his disapproval of his policy, and the danger he foresaw in the King's determination to bring the English Catholics to power. At Winchester once, in the Deanery garden, the King had asked him what people thought of the method he had adopted of 'touching' for the King's Evil. 'Why, truly,' Churchill replied, 'they show very little liking to it, and it is the general voice of your people that your Majesty is paving the way for the introduction of Popery.' The King was angry. 'How!' he exclaimed. 'Have I not given them my royal word, and will they not believe their King?' 'What I spoke, sir,' Churchill answered, 'proceeded purely from my zeal for your Majesty's service. But I have been bred a Protestant, and intend to live and die in that communion; above nine parts in ten of the whole people are of the same persuasion, and I fear (which excess of duty makes me say) from the genius of the English nation, and their natural aversion to the Roman Catholic worship, some consequences which I dare not so much as name, and which it creates in me a horror to think of.' Those were plain words, and bold ones. They came as near to a direct warning as the relationship of the two men permitted.

All this, however, is to anticipate the story. The last few years of Charles II's reign were for Churchill and his wife the calmest that they were destined to have. There was no immediate prospect of war, and Churchill was eager to withdraw as much as he could from active politics. He settled with Sarah on a property which had belonged to her family near St Albans, and built the house called Holywell (demolished after his death), which was to remain his principal home until, in the closing years of life, he went to live in the half-finished palace of Blenheim. He was in high favour at Court, both with his patron the Duke and with the King – with whom he would play tennis, that game of kings. Two daughters were born, Henrietta in 1681, Anne three years later. Churchill would have liked at this time to withdraw his wife entirely from the Court, and would doubtless have done so, but for an event which was to have important consequences. This was the marriage in 1683 of James's daughter, the Princess Anne, to Prince George of Denmark.

The princess was four years younger than Sarah, and they had met as children at the Court of St James. From the beginning a strong affection had sprung up between them, and grew with the years. On Anne's side, at any rate, it was strangely intense. She was to give her husband – the father of her sixteen children, of whom not one survived – her duty, loyalty, and affection; but her love was for Sarah. It was only natural that, when she married, she would want Sarah to be at hand. Sarah, for her part, was willing enough, and accepted the proffered appointment of Lady of the Bedchamber. The Princess and her husband were settled in a house called the Cockpit, adjoining the Palace of Westminster. To this arrangement Churchill made no objection, and as time went on his growing devotion to Anne, first as Princess and afterwards as Queen, was, in its chivalry and strength, one of the chief marks of a character essentially noble. Throughout her young womanhood, filled as it was with so much grief, and with the future never sure, he was her chief protector and guide, and the immense services he rendered her as Queen were touched by something of the romantic light, which, for the seamen of a less sophisticated age, had shone upon Elizabeth.

The accession of James II, who had been Churchill's patron for the past nineteen years, opened to him the prospect of further advancement. His position as a Protestant servant of a Catholic King was not an easy one, but for a short time at any rate he was encouraged, like everyone else, by James's promises to respect the established religion and constitution of the country. After the coronation he was raised to the English peerage, as Baron Churchill of Sandridge, and it was not long before he was able to prove his loyalty to the new King by his defeat at Sedgemoor of the rebel Duke of Monmouth. Unhappily, however, Monmouth's rebellion, with its bloody aftermath of hangings, was the signal for an ominous change in the King's behaviour, and his true purpose was revealed. Lord Churchill made no secret of how he stood: 'If the King', he declared to Lord Galway, 'should attempt to change our religion and constitution, I will instantly quit his service.' He and Sarah, with their trusted friend Godolphin, persuaded Princess Anne to consent to abandon her father, should the need arise, rather than her religion; and, as has already been noted, Churchill uttered the gravest of warnings to the King himself. The introduction of four Catholic peers into the Privy Council, the arbitrary Declaration of Indulgence, the raising of a new army under Catholic officers, the King's determination, no longer concealed, to force upon England a Catholic and autocratic government after the model of the French, and, finally, the birth of a Prince of Wales which brought with it the plain threat that James's courses would not end with his death: all this at length decided Churchill to use the influence he possessed in helping to bring about the Revolution. He wrote to William, promising his support: 'My places and the King's favour I set at nought, in comparison of being true to my religion. In all things but this the King may command me'; and in the same letter he told William that Princess Anne had come to the same resolution. Again, on the eve of William's coming: 'My honour I take leave to put into your Highness's hands, in which I think it safe' – 'it is what I owe to God and my country'. Thus the basis was laid for Churchill's betrayal of his master – if betrayal it was. Even James himself might have foreseen it. The bloodless Revolution took place and William was accepted as the new sovereign; the extreme violence of party strife was allayed; the dawn of religious toleration began; the long struggle between King and Parliament was replaced by cooperation between them. Two days before the coronation of William and Mary Lord Churchill was created Earl of Marlborough.

Marlborough was now sent to the Netherlands to command the British forces, which were once again engaged against France. His success at Walcourt won the praise of the King, and the next year he followed William's victory in Ireland at the battle of the Boyne by the capture of Cork and Kinsale, two strongholds in the hands of the exiled James's supporters. Nevertheless he was not yet assured of the King's confidence. William's position during the early years of his reign was delicate and difficult. He was a foreigner, and had little love for the English, just as the English had little love for him, and were jealous of the Dutchmen he raised to power; James, the hereditary king, seemed less wicked absent than present; Jacobite sentiment was strong, and at any moment a counter-revolution might come. Marlborough was in correspondence with the exiled Court, and possibly William was aware of the fact; at any rate he knew how close the association between James and Marlborough had formerly been. Moreover, Marlborough was in the innermost councils of Princess Anne, with whom her sister, Queen Mary, had bitterly quarrelled; and the possibility was always present to the King's mind of a movement, led by Marlborough at the head of the troops, to put Anne upon the throne in his place. The outcome was that Marlborough was without warning dismissed from all his appointments, and, soon afterwards, flung into the Tower on a charge of high treason. Fortunately, however, both for him and for England, the only direct evidence against him turned out to be a forgery. The incident would not be worth mentioning except for the light it throws upon the sort of atmosphere in which politics were conducted. William, however, with his strong good sense, was willing, as his tenure of the throne became in the course of time more secure, to employ a number of men whom he knew to have engaged in secret communications with the Court at St Germain. Marlborough, his ablest soldier, was amongst them, and the King marked his renewed confidence by making Marlborough, after six years' exclusion from state affairs, Governor to Princess Anne's nine-year-old son, the Duke of Gloucester and presumptive heir to the throne, who nevertheless, like all Anne's children, was soon to die. 'Teach him', said the King, 'to be like yourself, and he will not want accomplishments.'

Then, in 1701, the King sent Marlborough to the Continent to conclude the alliance between England, Holland, and the Empire, and to draw subsequently into the confederacy as many of the German States and principalities as he could. It was a mission of the highest importance. William perhaps already knew that he would not live to fight the coming campaign; he was bequeathing the task to the only man capable of carrying it out.

Marlborough and the King had one great purpose in common, the defeat of France. It was this that in the last years of William's reign drew the two men together, and finally overcame the suspicion and reserve which the King had so long felt for his greatest servant. Marlborough's ability as a soldier he had long recognized; in Flanders once, in 1691, the Prince of Vaudemont, being asked his opinion of the English generals, replied: 'I have lost my wonted skill in physiognomy, if any subject of your Majesty can ever attain such a height of glory as the Earl of Marlborough'; and the King answered: 'Cousin, you have done your part in answering my question; and I believe the Earl of Marlborough will do his to verify your prediction.' But Marlborough had still ten years to wait before he was given the chance to do so. The waiting was hard, but he was a patient man. Often the close-knit circle of friends at the Cockpit – Marlborough and Sarah, the Princess Anne and the Lord Treasurer Godolphin – would look forward to the time when Anne would be Queen, and Marlborough come into his own. That 'sunshine day' – the phrase was Anne's – would surely dawn. And when it did dawn, Marlborough assumed his immense responsibilities with the blessing of the dying King, who almost with his last words commended him to his successor as the man of all Englishmen best fitted to serve her.

When William died, Marlborough was fifty-two. He had four daughters and one son, who was to die of small-pox when he was only sixteen the following year, to his father's lasting grief. Time had left its mark upon Marl-borough; but character, though it may develop, does not change, and there still lived in the man of fifty-two the boy who from his earliest years had set himself resolutely to escape from poverty, and to build a fortune as amongst the surest ways to build his fame. He was an earl, but the poorest man of his rank in the country; in order to found a family which should take its proper place amongst the noble families of England – one of his and Sarah's dearest ambitions – it was still necessary to acquire money and to save it. He lived with the utmost frugality; he was said to have but three coats, and he kept account of every penny he spent. He seldom entertained. There are many stories of his parsimony: once at cards with Lord Bath he lost some money and had to borrow sixpence to pay for a chair to take him home. Lord Bath, having lent him the sixpence, said to his brother, who was present: 'I will wager any sum you please the Duke will now walk home.' And the Duke did. In an age of lavish expenditure it is not surprising that he should have acquired a reputation for meanness; but to balance the gossip of his contem-poraries, one should remember that to save his father from debt he forwent, as a young man, his reversionary interest in the small family estate, that he was uniformly generous to his junior officers in the army (he once made one a present of £1,000 to enable him to buy his pro-motion), and that he refused an heiress in order to marry for love. He was niggardly only in his own plea-sures. His personal charm even his enemies admitted. 'His address is most courteous,' wrote the Dutchman Goslinga; 'and while his handsome and well-graced countenance engages everyone in his favour at first sight, his perfect manners and his gentleness win over even those who start with a prejudice against him.' To subordinates he was always considerate: 'He could not chide a servant,' a friend said of him, 'and was the worst served possible, and in command he could not give a harsh word, no not to the meanest sergeant or corporal or soldier.' Trained from youth as a diplomat, he had all the arts of diplomacy: keen judgement of men, unruffled self-possession, patience, and an extraordinary grasp of the complex of forces which set the political scene. He was never a popular figure, as Nelson was, and he never courted popularity. Indeed, when Marlborough lived, it was still dangerous for a subject to become too great. Where Nelson glowed, Marlborough was cool. Nelson went into battle with the ardour and ecstasy of a lover. Marlborough controlled the moves of the game with the calm concentration of a chess-player. Nelson had two loves, his country and his mistress; Marlborough had only one – Sarah. Yet he was as great a patriot; the supreme purpose of his life, to raise England to that pre-eminence in the world which was to last for over two hundred years, he pursued with stubborn and unflinching tenacity. But he could write to Sarah before his march to the Danube and the battle of Blenheim, 'I do from my soul wish we could retire and not be blamed'. He knew well enough where his work lay; but his heart was at home.

One of the first acts of Queen Anne after her accession was to confer the Garter upon Marlborough, to make him Captain-General of the armies at home and abroad, and Master-General of the Ordnance. With the complete confidence of the Queen, and with his friend Godolphin in control of the Treasury, he was the most powerful man in England.

For eight years of William's reign England in alliance

with Holland, Spain, and the German States had been at war with France. For the greater part of this period Marlborough had had no command. When an indecisive peace was concluded at Ryswick in 1697, each side was in much the same position as when the fighting had begun. In spite of the powerful combination which William had raised against her, France held her own. When, however, the war was renewed four years later, almost all the advantages were on the side of France. By the death of the King of Spain and the proclamation of Louis XIV's grandson as his successor, the whole Spanish inheritance in Europe passed into French control; Milan and Naples became, for fighting purposes, French territory; all the fortresses of the Spanish Netherlands, which William had spent years in taking or trying to take, admitted French troops without a blow. The great state of Bavaria went over to the French cause, and Austria was weakened by the insurrection of her Hungarian subjects. Louis, in fact, was master of Europe, and the threat to Holland and England was imminent and deadly. The only advantage which France did not possess was, happily for England, sea-power – and she had no commander capable of waging a world war with the strategic genius of Marlborough. It was that genius which turned the scale, and at the end of the ten years of bitter fighting under Marlborough's leadership, England was to emerge as the dominant power in Europe, mistress of the seas – including the Mediterranean – and without a commercial rival in the world.

Throughout William's campaigns, Marlborough, watching from England, must have fretted against the lack of vision with which they were conducted. He knew that a great war could never be won by a succession of petty sieges; if any permanent result was to be attained, a war of movement must be set on foot and the French armies sought out, brought to battle, and destroyed. To assist in bringing about this result, the British fleet must control the Mediterranean, and thus complete the encirclement of the continental enemy. He was the first Englishman to comprehend the strategy of world war, and in his intuitive grasp of it he has never been surpassed before the two world wars of our own day. From the beginning, however, he was faced with grave difficulties, not from the enemy, but from his allies and his own countrymen.

It was the Whig party which had supported King William in his campaigns; but on the accession of Anne the Tories were returned to power. The Tories had, indeed, been brought over to support the renewal of the war, but their notions of how it should be waged were very different from Marlborough's. They were firmly opposed to venturing English armies on the Continent, and thought that England, as an island power, should confine herself to naval enterprise in pursuit of commerce and possessions overseas. But to venture English armies on the Continent was precisely what Marlborough wished, and intended, to do, knowing, as he did, that a thrust at the heart of the French power was the only way of bringing Louis XIV to his knees. The Dutch, too, England's most powerful allies, were loath to fight away from their frontiers, and saw the war chiefly in terms of Dutch security against French aggression behind their ring of fortresses and the protection of their dykes. Marlborough, therefore, had to persuade, hoodwink, or cajole not only his allies but even the Tory government in England, before he could make any one of the decisive moves which he knew were necessary for success. In view of this fact, the importance of the partnership between Marlborough and Godolphin becomes clear: Godolphin, bound to Marlborough by lifelong friendship and the closest political association, was Lord Treasurer, and could be counted upon to find the money for Marlborough's campaigns. Anyone else at the Treasury might have withheld supplies for any enterprise which did not suit the Tory conception of how the war should be fought, and so crippled Marlborough at the outset.

In the middle of May 1702, Marlborough sailed from Margate to take up his command. He left England with a heavy heart. Sarah saw him off, and when they had said good-bye, 'I could have given my life to come back', he wrote as the ship left the harbour, 'though I know my weakness so much that I durst not, for I knew I should have exposed myself to the company. I did, for a great while, with a perspective glass, look upon the cliffs, in hopes I might have had one sight of you.' And, two months later, he is thinking of the peaches in their garden at Holywell.

Armies in Marlborough's day did not have competent and elaborate staffs such as they have today; almost every detail of organization fell upon the commander; but in the press of multifarious business, made more irksome by the continual necessity of smoothing over the quarrels and jealousies of the allied leaders, Marlborough in poor health, suffering from violent headaches and sickness, and often compelled to be in the saddle for nine or ten hours a day, seldom let slip an opportunity at the day's end to write to Sarah. Again and again he expressed his longing to retire, to be free of business, and to live with her and the children at his beloved Holywell. But his work was not done: 'Believe this truth,' he wrote to Godolphin, 'that I honour and love you, my lady Marlborough, and my children, and would die for the Queen.'

The campaign of 1702, though successful, was not what Marlborough had hoped to make it. More than once he was prevented by the over-cautious Dutch from engaging the French army in the field; nevertheless he forced the enemy to withdraw from their line of fortresses on the Meuse and the Lower Rhine. On his return to England in the winter he was made a Duke.

The following year was more vexatious for the Commander-in-Chief, who by the dissensions of his allies was prevented from exercising real command. The new fact in the situation was the treachery of Bavaria; the defection of the Elector, Max Emmanuel, put a powerful additional force at the disposal of France in a vital field of the war. The threat to the Empire was obvious and immediate; and if the Empire fell, the whole Grand Alliance would collapse. The war had also spread to Spain, whither troops had to be diverted, and the French grip was closing on the Upper Rhine and the Moselle. The Dutch would do nothing; again Marlborough encountered their obstinate refusal to risk their armies in any decisive battle, even when the odds were in their favour – and without the Dutch the English troops were far too few. At home Marlborough was blamed for failures not his own, and for a moment he had thoughts of resigning his command. Perhaps he would have done so, had it not been for a direct appeal from the Queen; 'if you should ever forsake me,' she wrote in a famous letter (it was addressed to Sarah), 'I would have nothing more to do with the world, but make another abdication; for what is a crown when the support of it is gone?' After that, Marlborough thought no more of resignation; his mind was set upon new courses: somehow or other he must break the deadlock in the Netherlands, escape from the meshes in which he was entangled by Dutch obstruction and timidity, and strike a telling blow.

The greatest danger to the Allies in 1703 was the imminent collapse of Austria, which by the treachery of Bavaria had been brought so near. If Austria were forced to sign a separate peace, the Allied confederacy would disintegrate, and France would remain mistress of Europe and of the world. This was the dominant fact which led Marlborough to Blenheim. The Dutch, of course, would never consent to send their armies so far from home, so Marlborough determined to go without them: he would march with the troops in English pay alone, and have, for the first time, an army under his own sole control, free from the intolerable restrictions of the Dutch field deputies. Yet even to do this was no easy matter; for at the prospect of the Netherlands being suddenly denuded of English troops, the Dutch, not unnaturally, took alarm. Marlborough proceeded cautiously, veiling his real purpose; gradually and with his usual patience, he persuaded the Dutchmen that a campaign upon the Moselle would be necessary the following spring – but he said not a word about the Danube. Nevertheless, his plans were made: he would march to the Danube, join forces with the Margrave of Baden and Prince Eugene, and deliver Austria by a decisive blow. His Dutch allies – magnificent fighting men, but led by soldiers who had no conception of the war beyond the immediate defence of their own country – must be bamboozled for their own ultimate safety.

Early in May 1704, the march from Flanders began. By the 19th the army was approaching the Rhine. Four days later it became clear to the French that it was making for Coblenz, on the junction of the Rhine and the Moselle. What was its objective? The French commanders supposed that Marlborough intended a campaign on the Moselle, to clear the fortresses of Trarbach and Trèves. But they could not be sure. Villeroy started south from the Low Countries, to watch the Moselle. Tallard hurried north to Strasbourg, to watch the Rhine. Marshal Marsin and the Elector of Bavaria could not begin their intended assault upon Austria while the position in the north was still uncertain. Thus, from the day his march began, the initiative passed from the French, who, with their 'interior lines' of communication, might have launched an attack in any direction they pleased, to Marlborough.

Towards the end of the month Marlborough's army crossed to the right bank of the Rhine just above Coblenz – so there was to be no campaign on the Moselle after all. Slowly, deliberately, the scarlet column crept on towards the east, and still the French were kept guessing at its destination. It crossed the Main; and news came that bridges were being built over the Rhine, forty miles further on, by the Governor of Philippsburg – surely, then, the English objective was Alsace? But again the French were wrong. On June 3rd Marlborough crossed the Neckar, and at last it was no longer possible to conceal his design from the enemy: he turned east, and headed openly for the Danube.

Suddenly it was apparent to the French that the whole strategic situation had been turned against them. Marlborough's army, now hurrying south-east, would soon join the 50,000 troops which, under the command of the Margrave of Baden, were watching Marshal Marsin near Ulm. The French armies – Marsin's at Ulm, Villeroy's and Tallard's on the other side of the Rhine near Landau – were widely separated. Marlborough, with a superior force of some 100,000 men, could attack either of them separately and overwhelm them.

At the little town of Wiesloch near Heidelberg, on June 10th, Marlborough for the first time met Prince Eugene of Savoy, commander of the Austrian armies. On the instant, each recognized the other's quality, and rejoiced in the recognition. The most famous military partnership in history had begun. For Marlborough, who had so long been trammelled by the bickerings and petty jealousies of rival princes under his command, and the selfish timidity of the Dutch, the presence of Eugene was like a liberating wind. Here, at last, was a soldier who could see the pattern of the war with the same large vision as himself, a man who would fight at his side with a loyalty equal to his courage and skill.

Still the army moved on to the south-eastward, at a steady pace of a dozen miles a day. The men were in good heart and full of vigour: 'Money', Prince Eugene said, 'will buy clothes and fine horses, but it can't buy that lively air I see in every one of these troopers' faces.' By the end of the month Marlborough had joined forces with the Margrave near Ulm, and on July 1st the Schellenberg, a fortress on the Danube, was taken by storm after bitter fighting. The way was open for the invasion of Bavaria. Eugene meanwhile was a hundred miles away, watching the French armies under Villeroy and Tallard near Strasbourg on the Rhine. Riders kept Marlborough in constant touch with him, and when it was known, at the end of July, that Tallard was on the march towards Ulm in an attempt to relieve Marsin and the Elector, Eugene set out through the mountains to join the English force. The first great battle of the war was imminent.

There is not space here to describe in detail this memorable fight, which was fought on both sides with great gallantry, and on the Allied side with extraordinary skill. It was Marlborough's first major action between armies in the field, but he was already as great a master of tactics as of the larger strategy of war. Like Nelson, he had an intuitive knowledge of the place and moment at which to strike, and, like Nelson, he had the absolute confidence of his officers and men – and now too, as Nelson had his 'band of brothers', so Marlborough had, in Prince Eugene, the beloved comrade-in-arms, whose name was to be linked with his own in the memory of men for ever – 'two bodies and one soul'.

It was six in the morning on 13 August 1704 when the

French saw the Allied troops assembling beyond the little River Nebel, which runs into the Danube a mile and a half east of the village of Blenheim. They had not been expecting an attack. Their position was a strong one, occupying the whole four miles of plain between the Danube and the mountains to the north-west, so, even though they had been caught unawares, they were confident of success. But they did not yet know their opponents. Before the day ended their centre was broken, two thousand of their cavalry had been driven into the river to drown, twenty-seven battalions of infantry, shut up in Blenheim, had surrendered, and Marshal Tallard himself, with two other generals, had been taken prisoner. Marsin and the Elector of Bavaria escaped. At the crisis of the battle Marlborough, seeing the centre hard-pressed sent to Eugene on the right of the Allied line, to ask him to send as reinforcement the brigade of Imperial Cuirassiers. Eugene was himself in desperate danger, but he unquestioningly complied. The arrival of the Cuirassiers turned the scale.

No mention has been made of the Margrave in this battle; the reason is simple – the Margrave was not there. It is a curious comment upon the complexity of Marlborough's problems that he and Eugene had together taken delicate and tactful steps to get the Margrave, who was not to be trusted, out of the way. No mention of the impending battle was made to him, and he had been persuaded to undertake the siege of a town forty miles in the Allied rear. The poor Margrave was very indignant when he heard the news of the victory. Marlborough that day had been for seventeen hours on horseback; he found time at the end of it to scribble a note to Sarah – in pencil, on the back of a bill of tavern expenses.

The battle of Blenheim saved Austria and the Grand Alliance, and put a final stop to Louis XIV's ambition for conquest. Henceforward, though the war was to con-

tinue for another ten years, Louis had no thought but of
how to conclude a peace on the least unfavourable terms.
Malbrouck s'en va-t-en guerre: 'Malbrouck' had, indeed,
gone to war with some purpose; the immense prestige of
the French armies was broken. In the same year Gibraltar was taken by the British, to be followed in 1708 by
the capture of Port Mahon in Minorca; so another of
Marlborough's great designs, the control of the Mediterranean to bring about the encirclement of France, was
beginning to take shape.

When Marlborough returned to England at the close
of the campaign, the Queen granted him the Manor of
Woodstock and undertook to build for him, at her own
expense, the huge mansion of Blenheim Palace, where
his heirs still live today. He enjoyed his fame and his rich
rewards; commander-in-chief, bound to the Queen by
lifelong ties and in her innermost confidence, Prime
Minister in effect though not in name, he was now the
most powerful man in England; but unfortunately for
him – his work was not yet over.

The war continued, and everywhere success attended
Marlborough's arms. As Blenheim had saved Austria, so
Ramillies two years later saved the Netherlands, and
Oudenarde, in 1708, laid open to the Allied armies the
direct path for the invasion of France. By 1707 the major
objects of the war were already won: Louis XIV's ambition to dominate Europe was finally checked; his armies
had been broken at Ramillies and Turin; they had been
driven from Italy; Antwerp was in Allied hands, and
France was reduced to impotence upon the sea. Marlborough's influence with the States which composed the
Grand Alliance was supreme. It was the moment to make
peace; but peace was not made, and, when at last it
came seven years later, most of Marlborough's hard-won
gains were to be thrown away.

Just at the time when Marlborough's influence on the

Continent was at its highest, the foundation of his power at home began to crack: 'I will endeavour', he had written to Sarah after Blenheim, 'to leave a good name behind me in countries that have hardly any blessing but that of not knowing the detested names of whig and tory' – and there was reason enough for this outburst of anger. The Queen was a Tory, and the Tories, who up to now had been in power, had never supported Marlborough's war policy, though as Englishmen they welcomed his victories. It was the Whigs who in Anne's reign, as in William's, were the party of all-out war with France. Now, therefore, seeing the success of the Allied arms on the Continent, they were determined, as a party, to force themselves upon the Queen; if they failed, they would, by their majority in Parliament, ruin Godolphin as Lord Treasurer and by withholding supplies make it impossible for Marlborough to carry on the war. As the first step in their bid for power, Sunderland (who was Marlborough's son-in-law) was to be made Secretary of State. The Queen violently opposed this measure. She was a Stuart to her backbone, and abhorred the control of either party, especially the control of the hated Whigs, the party of Dissent, who cared little for her beloved Church, and were determined that the alien and detestable George of Hanover should succeed her on the throne. But relentless pressure was brought to bear: Sarah, her lifelong friend, lectured her day and night; Godolphin threatened resignation, and finally, Marlborough himself, knowing that the ability of the Grand Alliance to continue the war was at stake, bluntly informed the Queen by letter of what would happen if she refused: 'How is it possible', he wrote, 'to obtain near five millions for carrying on the war with vigour, without which all is undone?' Thus Marlborough, a Tory by birth and, for many years, by persuasion, was at last drawn by the necessity of events into the company of the Whigs. It was the end, both for him and Sarah, of the old, close intimacy with the Queen. Sarah's Whiggism Anne had tolerated for years, because she loved her; now Sarah had gone too far, and Marlborough himself, she could not but feel, had deserted her. Marlborough was still indispensable, and the Queen still listened to his counsel; but the old bond was broken. Sarah, for her part, had lost her place in the Queen's affection for ever, and was soon replaced by the notorious Abigail Masham, who was to play her part, and that no small one, by intrigue and malicious whisperings, in bringing about Marlborough's disgrace. A few months later the Queen was compelled by inexorable pressure from Marlborough and the Whigs to dismiss her minister Harley, who, with his confederate Henry St John, afterwards Lord Bolingbroke, lost no time in laying plans for his subsequent revenge. Marlborough was at the height of his splendour and power; but already the clouds were gathering.

Meanwhile the scope of the war itself had widened. The Whigs, having forced themselves into power, took up with increasing fervour the cry of 'No peace without Spain', which had first been uttered several years before: Spain, with all her possessions in Europe and the New World, must be torn from the grasp of the Bourbons. To insist upon that was to abandon all hope of an early peace. Yet after Oudenarde, peace on the best of terms might have been had for the asking. Louis XIV was beaten; his armies could no longer face in the field the armies which Marlborough led; he was driven to the defence of the frontiers of France. To Marlborough and Eugene it seemed that one more campaign might bring the Allies to Paris. But they were wrong: two things, clear enough to us who know the whole story, gave Louis heart to struggle on, when his enemies made no offer of peace. The first was the valour which the French have always shown in the defence of their own soil; the second was the knowledge, which Louis possessed, that Marlborough was no longer in the confidence of the Queen. Perhaps he could hold out until Marlborough fell – until the Tories, the Peace Party, returned to power in England. Louis's hopes, as the event showed, were justified.

Nevertheless, Marlborough made one serious effort for peace in 1708. The negotiations were secret and undertaken on his own responsibility. Louis refused, partly, perhaps, because he doubted Marlborough's sincerity, partly because the great fortress of Lille had just fallen and the acceptance of an armistice at such a moment of disaster would look too much like absolute surrender. But the fact that the proposal was made is important; for one of the heaviest charges brought against Marlborough by his enemies in England was that he was deliberately prolonging the war for his own profit. Nothing could be further from the truth. Everyone knows (and would know even if Aristotle had not told him) that to be content a man must employ such talent as he possesses 'along the lines of excellence'; and of course Marlborough found fulfilment in the exercise of his genius as diplomatist and soldier; but very little knowledge of human nature is required to understand that a passionate longing to be rid of courts and camps for ever was in no way inconsistent with the necessary exercise of his powers. If Marlborough's actions are not sufficient proof that he was not prolonging the war for his own profit, his letters are; hardly one was written to his wife or friends which did not contain some expression of his desire for rest; 'My sole thought,' he once exclaimed, 'after I shall have done my utmost to secure a good and durable peace, is to retire into private life.'

In 1709 peace came very near; but the chance was lost through the impossible demand that Louis XIV should assist in the overthrow of his own grandson, Philip V of Spain. Throughout the complex and protracted negotiations Marlborough showed himself opposed to this demand and eager to make peace upon such honourable and advantageous terms as could be got without it. He has been blamed for not using his power to force England and the Allies to end the war, when it could have been ended so easily; but the truth is that the power to do so was no longer his. His position at home was already precarious; he was no longer the maker of policy; he was only the most powerful instrument the Government possessed for carrying out their wishes. Thus the hope of peace vanished from a war-weary Europe, and Marlborough turned once more to the bitter business of trying to break the last desperate resistance of the French against invasion.

Only one more great battle was to be fought. After the dreadful victory of Malplaquet on 11 September 1709 – dreadful for its expense of blood: the Allied losses were 24,000, the French some 15,000 – it seemed indeed that the path to Paris was open. 'God Almighty be praised,' Marlborough wrote to Sarah the instant the fighting ceased, 'it is now in our powers to have what peace we please, and I may be pretty well assured of never being in another battle; but that nor nothing in this world' – he added – 'can make me happy if you are not kind.' That characteristic phrase addressed to the woman who had been his wife for thirty-four years, suggests, amid the continuous labour of battle and intrigue in which he had been so long involved, where the deep centre of his life lay. The nobility of men is not only in their public deeds.

Marlborough, however, was wrong; the path to Paris had not been opened by the costly defeat of Marshals Villars and Boufflers at Malplaquet. French resistance, far from being broken, was stiffened; Louis XIV, moreover, now knew that Marlborough had not only lost the favour of the Queen, but that his fall could not be much longer delayed. The Peace Party in England would soon be back in power. Could he hold out until the Grand Alliance should be robbed of the one man who had held it together through seven years of war – the one general whom his own could never face in the field without defeat? He thought he could; and he was right.

Meanwhile Harley's plans for revenge upon the Whigs were rapidly maturing. He had the ear of the Queen, who herself longed to restore the Tories to power. Harley knew that the first step in his secret battle must be to discredit Marlborough and ultimately to ruin him. A whispering campaign was set going: Marlborough, it was rumoured, was growing fat on the spoils of war; he was deliberately prolonging it when the country, burdened with taxation, longed for peace; he was throwing away English lives by the thousand, but was very careful never to risk his own. Worse than all, he was plotting treason – he would, in his own good time, bring his armies into England, seize the person of the Queen, and make himself a second Cromwell. There were plenty of people in England ready enough to listen to such tales, and Harley saw to it that all of them were carried by Abigail Masham to the Queen.

One by one the Whig ministers were dismissed, beginning with Sunderland. Then Godolphin went, and when Harley succeeded him as Treasurer, it became certain that the Tories would win the party struggle – and that France would be spared the ultimate ignominy of defeat. Never has a change of government in England been fraught with such consequences for Europe, and perhaps the world. Marlborough, watching events at home, continued to do his duty in the field as commander-in-chief; but the heart had gone out of things and he already felt that much of his work was to be wasted. Towards the

Queen he still preserved his old deep loyalty, that odd mixture of almost mystical devotion to her office and of tender protectiveness towards her as a woman; but he knew that her fanatical hatred of the Whigs would be her ruin, and told her so bluntly enough. As for her, though she continued for a while to pretend that her greatest soldier and life-long friend, the man who had raised her country to a pinnacle of power in the world never attained by her before, was still indispensable, she had nevertheless made up her mind that he must go. Had he not forced her into the hands of the detested Whigs, who were so determined to clip the wings of her royal authority? And was it not all too likely that Mrs Masham's whispered tales were true? The Whigs must go, and Marlborough with them; then she could be (in her own phrase) 'queen indeed'.

By the end of 1710 the Tories were in power, and bent upon making peace. At once the Press attack upon Marlborough was begun; the coffee-houses buzzed with the malignant calumnies of Swift and Defoe; the wretched Mrs Manley, in *The New Atlantis*, dug up, or invented, youthful indiscretions which Marlborough had committed, or was supposed to have committed, at the Court of Charles II long ago. The Press in those days was a stimulant, not an anodyne; the journals by their very fewness had the more power. Marlborough in the Netherlands was still in command, and the war dragged on. Then in the autumn of 1711, the Tory ministers, led by Harley and St John, concluded with France without Marlborough's knowledge preliminary agreements for peace. Their next step was to come to their final reckoning with Marlborough: if he would consent to the proposed terms, they were content to leave him without further molestation; if he refused, they were determined to break him. Marlborough, of course, refused; the terms, when they were divulged, caused violent dissensions amongst the Allies, and Marlborough saw that they threw away most of what he had gained in the long course of the war. Harley and St John proceeded swiftly; a report was put about that Marlborough was to be charged with malversation of public money; the old story that he – perhaps with the help of Eugene - was planning to seize the throne was repeated, more insistently, to the Queen, who, ready enough to act even without further urging from her ministers, dismissed the Duke from all his offices. She wrote the letter of dismissal with her own hand. 'I wish your Majesty', said Marlborough in his reply, 'may never find the want of so faithful a servant as I have always endeavoured to approve myself to you.' The comment of Louis XIV is worth remembering. 'The affair', he said, 'of the displacing the Duke of Marlborough will do all for us we desire.'

A few weeks later a formal charge of peculation was brought against Marlborough. The substance of the charge was that throughout the war he had misappropriated annually certain sums paid by the Contractor for the army bread and bread-wagons, and also the $2\frac{1}{2}$ per cent which was allowed to be deducted from the pay of foreign troops in British service. In all, a sum of some £200,000 was involved. Marlborough's defence was that the money had all been applied, according to precedent, to financing his Secret Service – which, in point of fact, had never before been so efficient. No proof of the charge was ever established, and the frivolity of it was exposed by the fact that Marlborough's successor in the command, the Duke of Ormonde, was, by the same government which had accused Marlborough of peculation, authorized to draw precisely the same sums from the same sources. Marlborough, like a good many other men in this workaday world, loved money and the power and consequence it brings. From earliest youth he was determined to make money, and did make it. Presents he would take with the greatest complacency, but he never took a bribe. He might have had four million French livres from Louis if, in 1708, he had succeeded in induc-ing the Allies to make a by no means disadvantageous peace; he treated the offer with the contempt it deserved. Twice he was offered the vice-royalty of the Netherlands with a salary of £60,000 a year; he refused, lest the Dutch should object and the Alliance be thereby weakened. There can be little doubt that his enemies, when he was dismissed, made every effort to find evidence of some kind, however doubtful, that he had been guilty in his long command of corruption or fraud; but they found none.

The desertion, after Marlborough's dismissal, by the British troops of their allies in the field, and the con-clusion of peace at Utrecht in the spring of 1713, do not belong to this story, for Marlborough had no part in either. He was a 'private man' now, and had got what he long desired, though the manner of getting it was bitter, and the taste of freedom must have been like ashes in his mouth. He left England, and was soon joined by Sarah, and together they travelled about Germany, where they spent some time at the Court of Hanover. Here he made very plain to the Elector on which side he stood with regard to the succession to the British throne; Marl-borough's relations with the House of Stuart had often been ambiguous and sometimes inscrutable; but through them all one of the great purposes of his life, the Protest-ant succession in England, had remained constant.

He returned to England the day after the Queen's death, on 2 August 1714. It was a calmer England than he had left just over a year before, for the peril of civil war which might have come if Bolingbroke's Jacobite schemes had had time to mature, was averted by the sudden death of Queen Anne. King George I was pro-claimed without a struggle, and when he came to his new kingdom the following month, he reinstated Marl-borough as Captain-General of the army and Master of the Ordnance. But Marlborough was now an old man and fortunately had no more battles to fight. The last years of his life were spent partly at Holywell, partly at Windsor Lodge, and partly in the still unfinished palace of Blenheim. Early in the June of 1722 at Windsor Lodge he had a paralytic stroke – the last of three. For a few days he lingered, his mind still clear. He died at dawn on June 16th, in his seventy-third year.

Sarah survived him by twenty-two years, which were all devoted to his memory. When her husband died, she, at sixty-two, was still beautiful, still pulsing with her old, invincible vitality. The Duke of Somerset asked her to marry him, and her noble answer is perhaps Marl-borough's best epitaph. 'If', she declared, 'I were young and handsome as I was, instead of old and faded as I am, and you could lay the empire of the world at my feet, you should never share the heart and hand that once belonged to John, Duke of Marlborough.'

Keats

POETRY, like religion and philosophy, is one of the avenues along which men from time immemorial have tried to approach the still heart of life, to see the glow and feel the pulse of it, steady and reassuring, under the distracting and kaleidoscopic dazzle and change of circumstance and the evanescence of immediate pleasure or pain. By saints the central stillness is won in what they suppose to be union with God; by philosophers in what they believe to be truth; by poets in what they know to be beauty – three things which are perhaps aspects of the same reality. Poets, however, differ from saints and philosophers in that the road they follow leads them not, as with saints and philosophers, away from the common and familiar earth, but right through the middle of it; they are concerned with everything to be found there; nature and the human heart are the books which they must read. The saint escapes from the world into the ecstasy of his communion with God; the poet on the contrary lays himself open to its influences, and shows it to us transfigured by his own passionate contemplation and love. His concern, unlike the philosopher's, is not to discover the unfamiliar, but to irradiate the familiar; he does not seek to know, but is content to adore, and he is without defences against the slings and arrows of human suffering. Few poets have been happy men, as one commonly understands that word; but the greatest of them have, one and all, been something better; for they have never run away from experience, or grown a shell to protect themselves against its inevitable anguish, and thus, like lesser men, forfeited also their capacity for joy.

Keats was no exception; two years before he died, he wrote in a letter to his brother: 'The common cognomen of this world among the misguided and the superstitious is a "vale of tears" from which we are to be redeemed by a certain arbitrary interposition of God and taken to Heaven. What a little circumscribed straitened notion! Call the world if you please the "vale of soul-making" – then you will find out the use of the world.... Do you not see how necessary a world of pains and troubles is to school an intelligence and make it a Soul?' The story of Keats's short life, so well known to us not only from the poems which are, as it were, a hieroglyphic commentary upon it, but also from his own incomparable letters and from accounts of him written by his many friends, is the story of how he came to realize this. It is a story with little incident, but rich in adventures of the spirit on seas more perilous than those Columbus sailed, and in victories of mind and heart more permanent and rewarding than Trafalgar or the battle of the Nile. 'I am certain of nothing,' he once wrote, 'but of the truth of Imagination and the holiness of the heart's affections'; for that alone, had he told us nothing else and written no poetry, we should be in his debt for ever.

The Keats family came originally from the West country, possibly from Devon, more probably from Dorset. It was not a distinguished family. The poet's father, Thomas Keats, came up to London as a young man and was employed as head ostler in a livery-stable in Finsbury. Later he married his master's daughter and, on the master's retirement, was given the management of the business. The couple lived for a time at the stables, and there, at the sign of the Swan and Hoop, Finsbury Pavement, on 29 October 1795, John Keats was born. He was the eldest of a family of four – three boys and a girl. Between the brothers and the little sister, who was nearly eight years younger than John, there was a very strong bond of affection. When John was nine, his father was killed by a fall from his horse; six years later, while he was still at school, his mother, whom he loved passionately, died of consumption. During her brief illness, he would sit up whole nights with her, and allow no one but himself to give her her medicine or to cook her food. The children's grandmother, Mrs Jennings, lived for a few years longer and, wishing to make the best provision she could for her orphan grandchildren, put them under the care of a guardian, a tea-merchant named Abbey, who was also to hold in trust for them the greater part of the property which had come to Mrs Jennings under her late husband's will. Abbey's first act was to remove John from school, just before his sixteenth birthday, and bind him apprentice to a surgeon, Mr Thomas Hammond of Edmonton, to put him in the way of earning a living.

Keats's childhood, before the shadow first of his father's death and then of his mother's fell upon it, was a happy and natural one, warmed by family affection and filled with the common pleasures of the brooks and meadows of the English countryside, such as continued in later years to give an added grace to his poetry. He was small in stature – never more than a trifle over five feet – but well-built and strong, and of great personal beauty. His hair was red-brown and abundant, and soft 'as a bird's feathers', as one friend recalled; his eyes hazel-brown and brilliant 'with an inward look', his mouth mobile and expressive. His temperament was violent and explosive, quickly moved to rage, or pity, or laughter – always in extremes. He was a great fighter, seeking every occasion for a rough-and-tumble and thoroughly enjoying it when it came: it was 'meat and drink' to him, as a friend described it. Once, in school, an usher boxed his brother Tom's ears, and John, in a passion of anger, squared up to him and would have struck him. His rages were ungovernable; often his brother George would hold him down by main force when he was in 'one of his moods'; nor were his fits of hilarity less outrageous. The recital of a generous act would move him to tears. Sport and active exercise were a delight to him; at the same time – as all passions or aptitudes raised to a high pitch carry with them their opposites, like shadows – he was subject to fits of morbid melancholy and depression, to himself inexplicable and communicated to no one but his two beloved brothers. Men have to learn to master their temperaments as musicians have to learn to master their instruments; a violin is more difficult to play upon than a tin whistle, but, once brought under control, makes nobler music.

Keats was lucky in his school. He went to it when he was nine and was at once befriended by Charles Cowden Clarke, a boy some eight years older than himself and the headmaster's son. It was Clarke who first introduced him to the pleasures of reading and made him aware of his own vocation for poetry. The change – he appears to have had no particular interest in books until he was fourteen or so – came quite suddenly during his last few terms at school, and, as was to be expected with a boy who could do nothing by halves, it was violent and complete. Having begun to read, he read incessantly, morning, noon, and night, including meal-times; he went clean through the school library, devouring books of history, voyages, and travel, and appearing, as Clarke has recorded, to *learn by heart* the classical dictionary of Lemprière, and other works which dealt with the legends of ancient Greece. He learnt no Greek, but a little Latin – enough for him to make a prose version of Virgil's *Aeneid*.

His being taken from school so young, and just when his imagination was beginning to find the food it needed, might have had disastrous consequences, but for the fortunate chance that Edmonton, where Dr Hammond's practice was situated, was only a couple of miles from the Enfield school. Thus in the intervals of work under his new master, Keats was able to revisit his old school; this he did constantly, and under Clarke's able and sympathetic guidance began to make acquaintance with poetry. It was an intense and crucial experience, the opening of a new and marvellous world – almost as if, like Adam, he had awakened from a dream and found it true. In poetry, which he now read almost exclusively, all the turbulence of the young spirit within him, with its exaltations and despairs, its quick and delicate responses, its passionate idealism and generosity, found its justification and its balm. Poetry became for him, as it always remained, the only world in which the contradictions of experience were resolved, and with his delight in it came the realization that he, too, was destined, by a compulsion of his nature far deeper than mere predilection or whim, to be himself a poet. Passion and power will out; nevertheless, so subtle is the interplay between character and circumstance, that it is not difficult to imagine that without the assistance of Charles Cowden Clarke, coming as it did at this most impressionable period of Keats's adolescence, Keats – who had so short a time to live – might have missed his vocation.

Meanwhile his medical studies were proceeding well enough. His vitality and charm made him an agreeable companion, and friends have left on record that in spite of his inner preoccupation with poetry – which he was beginning secretly and tentatively to write – he was as well able as other young men to amuse himself with frivolities. Just before his twentieth birthday he left Edmonton and went to London as a student in the hospitals. A little more than a year later he was examined by the Court of Apothecaries and granted a licence to practise. In the spring of 1817 he abandoned medicine altogether and decided to devote himself wholly to

poetry. After leaving Edmonton he had lived in various
London lodgings: the first was in the Borough, 'a beastly
place in dirt, turnings, and windings', which made him
look back with longing to his boyhood days, on holiday
at his grandmother's house when he would amuse himself with 'Goldfinches, Tomtits, Minnows, Mice, Tickle-
backs, Dace, Cock salmons, and all the whole tribe of
the Bushes and the Brooks', and to his walks as a schoolboy
in the neighbourhood of Epping Forest, the Hampstead
hills and the rich countryside about Enfield Chase – 'But
might I now', he wrote in a rhyming letter to his friend
Mathew,

> each passing moment give
> To the coy muse, with me she would not live
> In this dark city –

then, with three fellow-students, he settled in St Thomas
Street; then with his brothers in the Poultry, and, lastly,
still with his brothers, in Cheapside. He has left us, in his
verse, a few glimpses of those days: of a November evening, for instance, when

> Small busy flames play through the fresh laid coals,
> And their faint cracklings o'er our silence creep
> Like whispers of the household goods that keep
> A gentle empire o'er fraternal souls;

or of occasional escapes from the murk of London into
the fields, when

> To one who has been long in city pent,
> 'Tis very sweet to look into the fair
> And open face of heaven – to breathe a prayer
> Full in the smile of the blue firmament –

unsure, tentative verse, but deeply touching to us who
know what was so soon to come. The most important
event, however, which took place during this period, was
his introduction to Leigh Hunt, a man who was at the

very heart of the new movement in contemporary literature. Hunt, who was eleven years older than Keats, had been in prison for publishing a libel on the Prince Regent; he was an indefatigable journalist, an acute and generous-minded critic, a stimulating talker, and a lover of civil and political liberty; he was also a poet of great fluency and, in his somewhat unbuttoned and boudoir manner, of not inconsiderable charm. Keats was soon to see the very obvious faults of Hunt's poetry, but at the moment Hunt's companionship and encouragement were invaluable to him. It was Cowden Clarke who brought the two together, having first sent to Hunt some specimen's of Keats's verses. Thereafter they were constantly together at the little house in the Vale of Health; the talk they had, upon every subject under the sun, but especially of literature, music, and painting –

> the pleasant flow
> Of words on opening a portfolio –

the walks over the Hampstead hills, and the long evenings and nights over the fire, when

> the chimes
> Of friendly voices had just given place
> To as sweet a silence,

were meat and drink to Keats's swiftly expanding intellect, as fighting had been to the exuberant animal spirits of his boyhood. Moreover, it is important to remember that this was an exciting time for anyone who cared for literature; powerful new currents were flowing and the ice of the long-accepted eighteenth-century forms was fast melting: Wordsworth and Coleridge, some eighteen years before, had produced the great challenge of their *Lyrical Ballads*; Scott had written his lays of the Border and the Highlands, Byron his romantic tales of Greece and the Levant; Wordsworth's *Excursion* had appeared in 1814. Poetry was embarked upon a new adventure of the spirit into regions very remote from the fashionable urban society which it was accustomed to frequent during the fifty years or more that Alexander Pope was king. Moreover, people read it – and there were even fortunes to be made from it, as by Byron and Tom Moore. Of these regions Keats was born a denizen, and his increasingly conscious realization of the fact, as he talked with Hunt, who was perfectly at home there, was as vivid an awakening into truth as his first readings of Spenser and the Elizabethans with Cowden Clarke had been. He began to write more, and to show what he had written. A sonnet of his was printed by Hunt in his journal, the *Examiner*. He was taken to visit the painter Haydon, and by that fiery enthusiast and genius *manqué* was initiated into the art of ancient Greece. The world of medicine and the hospitals took on in his thoughts an ever-increasing unreality – though his hand, it should be remembered, was skilful: 'My last operation', he was later to tell a friend, 'was the opening of a man's temporal artery. I did it with the utmost nicety; but reflecting on what passed through my mind at the time, my dexterity seemed a miracle.' The nature of those thoughts is not hard to imagine. Other contacts, other friendships followed – in particular with John Hamilton Reynolds, himself a writer of promise and a man to whom Keats could always open his heart, as his later letters were to show; and with the artist Joseph Severn, who was destined to perform for Keats a harder and more loving service than any other of his friends. Shelley he met, but did not take to. One result of this widening circle of friends, whose interests all chimed with his own, was to crystallize in him the determination to

do the deed
Which his own soul had to itself decreed,

and abandon his life to the pursuit of poetry. Accordingly, with the encouragement of everyone he knew, including his brothers, he decided, early in the year 1817, when he already had enough verses written to make a small volume, to inform his guardian Mr Abbey that he had turned his back upon his medical career for ever. Mr Abbey prudently objected, but his objections fell upon deaf ears. The decision was irrevocable. What Keats might have been, had he made for himself a career as a practising – and successful – surgeon no one can know; but from this moment it was ordained that he should become, as he once called Shakespeare, a 'miserable and mighty poet of the human heart'.

In view of that phrase, 'a miserable and mighty poet of the human heart', it is worth while to pause a moment and consider how Keats at this time, just before his first book was published, appeared to the people who knew him. He was very far from being miserable; on the contrary, he had an insatiable appetite for life, and boundless delight in every manifestation of it – even to watching a bear-baiting. Unlike Shelley, who seemed always to remember his exile from another and more radiant world – some

> loftiest star of unascended heaven
> Pinnacled dim in the intense inane –

Keats loved and identified himself with what was before his eyes and under his feet: the gentle English scene with its woods and hills and streams, and the infinite goings-on of men. Warm-hearted, affectionate, and tolerant, averse to the rigidity of dogma or creed, he could be moved to indignation only by injustice or meanness. Severn has recorded many memories of him at this time: of his delighted awareness of everything about him – clouds, wind in the trees, the rustling of small creatures in the hedgerows, the clothes and faces of passing vagrants,

wind again (which never failed to move him) sweeping
in waves across a barley-field; of his appearance – seem-
ing, as he did, taller than he was by the 'characteristic
backward poise' of the head, and a 'peculiarly dauntless
expression such as may be seen on the face of some seamen'; and of his manner in company, sometimes eagerly
talking in his low, rich voice, sometimes abstracted and
silent, sometimes riotous with laughter or amusing his
friends with mimicry. The extreme sensibility which is a
constant element in an impassioned nature such as his,
was not, indeed, even at this happy period, to be without
its effect upon him; but it was apt, as yet, to find its
expression in pleasure rather than in pain; the fits of
melancholy and despondence were still no more than an
undercurrent beneath the bright surface of a life of vivid
and exhilarating experience. He had, moreover, the
precious faculty of admiration, amounting to hero-
worship, not only for great men of the past, but – which
is rarer – for his contemporaries. Feeling as he did that
England was on the threshold of a great resurgence of the
human spirit, which would

> give the world another heart
> And other pulses,

he was full of reverence for the men whom he felt to be
leading the way. When Haydon mentioned his intention
of showing Wordsworth a sonnet which Keats had
written, 'the idea', Keats replied, 'put me out of breath.
You know with what reverence I would send my well-
wishes to him.' Already conscious of the awakening
power within himself, confident of ultimate success in
his chosen vocation and possessing a grasp of life and an
intellectual balance far beyond his years, he nevertheless
had one deep-seated cause of self-mistrust – he was not at
ease in the company of women. He could, indeed, joke
with Reynolds's sisters as if they were his own, and, when

his brother George became engaged, he was genuinely and deeply devoted to his future sister-in-law; but, when the relationship was neither, on the one hand, deliberately light, nor, on the other, clearly defined by its own nature, he seems to have been uneasy. When he did, finally, fall in love, it was to be not a fulfilment but an agony, and to hasten his death. In this alone he failed to reach the ideal by the only certain way – which is the full understanding and acceptance of the real.

As a motto for his 1817 volume Keats chose Spenser's lines:

> What more felicity can fall to creature
> Than to enjoy delight with liberty?

and these butterfly words suit well enough the quick and delicate awareness of the varied beauty of the physical world, which provides the substance of much of what the volume contains. One poem, however – *Sleep and Poetry* – is of especial interest and importance in any sketch of Keats as a person rather than as a poet – if for a moment one may make the distinction. In this poem he expresses for the first time his own noble idea of what poetry is, or might be: an idea, incidentally, which was at the root of the new movement which had already broken the old conception of eighteenth-century verse.

> A drainless shower
> Of light [he wrote] is poetry; 'tis the supreme of power;
> 'Tis might half-slumbering on its own right arm.

Poetry, he felt, was not, as the two preceding generations had come to believe, an intellectual pleasure or cultivated accomplishment: it was a way of penetrating to the ultimate mystery of human life – not a garland to adorn it, but a power to mould it. In poetry, the beat and tremble of divine wings awakened a response from something in men which is older and deeper than the know-

ledge painfully acquired through the centuries by the
processes of thought. Poets, in Keats's eyes, were the true
heroes, the men of power who were the source of all
that is finest in the life of the world. The mere hope that
he might one day join their company filled him with a
kind of awe – and yet, with one half of himself, he already
knew that that was his destiny. True pride and true
humility are extremes which meet – and neither is
possible without forgetfulness of self. With a wisdom
and clarity of judgement extraordinary in a young man
of twenty-one, Keats knew exactly what he was, and
what – given the opportunity – he had the power to
become.

> O Poesy – for thee I hold my pen,
> That am not yet a glorious denizen
> Of thy wide heaven;

and again, in the same poem,

> Oh for ten years, that I may overwhelm
> Myself in poesy; so I may do the deed
> That my own soul has to itself decreed.

No poet yet – nothing much better than a 'pet-lamb in a
sentimental farce', as he wryly described himself in
thinking of the easy flattery that such friends as Hunt
and Haydon lavished upon a promising boy – but conscious, nevertheless, of what he could be, if only he were
given time. Moreover, he already knew, with a kind of
intuitive prevision, the nature of the road which he
would have to travel in order to 'do his deed'. Few
things are more interesting than his account of this road
in *Sleep and Poetry*, one of the earliest of his poems; for it
shows us the germ of an idea which never left him –
which grew to a bud in *Endymion*, and finally flowered
in the two incomparable fragments of *Hyperion*, the
second of which was written just before illness silenced

him for ever. There is not space here for much quotation, but the idea is briefly this: high poetry demands knowledge; knowledge involves suffering, which the poet must not merely submit to, but actively and willingly embrace, in order to transcend it and so arrive at the wisdom which is beyond the partial conception of good and evil. Thus there are three stages in the growth of a poet: first his immediate and unthinking response to beauty, unburdened with speculation or doubt; then his entry into, and sharing of, the dark and tormented world of human passion; and finally – the supreme achievement – the carrying over of the first into the second, so that beauty itself is clothed in graver and richer colours. In *Sleep and Poetry* two only of these stages are described, the third merely hinted at. Nearly two years later he recurred to the subject in a famous letter: 'I compare human life', he wrote, 'to a large Mansion of many apartments, two of which I can only describe, the doors of the rest being as yet shut upon me. The first we step into we call the Infant, or Thoughtless Chamber, in which we remain as long as we do not think. We remain there a long while, and notwithstanding the doors of the second Chamber remain wide open, showing a bright appearance, we care not to hasten to it; but are at length imperceptibly impelled by the awakening of the thinking principle within us – we no sooner get into the second Chamber, which I shall call the Chamber of Maiden Thought, than we become intoxicated with the light and the atmosphere, we see nothing but pleasant wonders, and think of delaying there for ever in delight. However, among the effects this breathing is father of is that tremendous one of sharpening one's vision into the heart and nature of Man – of convincing one's nerves that the world is full of Misery and Heartbreak, Pain, Sickness and oppression – whereby this Chamber of Maiden Thought becomes gradually darkened, and at

the same time, on all sides of it, many doors are set open –
but all dark – all leading to dark passages. We see not
the balance of good and evil; we are in a mist . . . we feel
the "Burden of the Mystery". To this point was Wordsworth come when he wrote "Tintern Abbey", and it
seems to me that his genius is explorative of those dark
Passages. Now if we live, and go on thinking, we too
shall explore them.' Keats did explore them, to the end;
and the supreme expression of what he found there is –
explicitly – in the two fragments of *Hyperion*, and –
implicitly – in two or three of the great odes. Meanwhile
as the poems of the 1817 volume were being written,
the Chamber of Maiden Thought still held him, and
his muse was a butterfly in a flower-garden, sipping
sweets.

The little volume was a failure; apart from a wise and
generous notice by his friend Hunt in the *Examiner*, it
was totally ignored. One angry purchaser brought his
copy back to the booksellers and declared it was 'no
better than a take-in'. Keats was hurt, but not dis-
couraged. He was to be worse hurt later; but he was
always his own severest critic, fully aware of the gap
between aim and achievement and, though he was as
sensible of genuine praise as any man, the immortal
part of him – if one may use the expression – did not
care twopence for public opinion. The familiar legend
that he was killed by the reviews is nonsense.

In the early spring of this same year Keats left his
brothers in London and went off on his own to the Isle of
Wight – to begin a new poem. Having found lodgings in
Carisbrooke, he set to work without delay, his thoughts in
a fever. 'I find', he wrote, 'I cannot exist without poetry
– without eternal Poetry – half the day will not do – the
whole of it – I began with a little, but habit has made me
a Leviathan.' The breathless sentences image his mood.
He wore himself out and could not sleep, so that in a

week or so he became, as he put it, 'not over capable in his upper stories', adding that the solitude weighed upon him and drove him in consequence to be 'in a continual burning of thought, as an only resource'. He moved to Margate and got his youngest brother Tom to join him. The new poem went on fast – he had set himself a time limit within which to finish it, as if, with the self-knowledge which was characteristic of him, he was aware that it was to be a task merely, of little importance in itself but necessary as a stage upon the road he must travel. The quality of the poem – it was *Endymion* – was best described by Shelley, who read it, as he said, 'with ever new sense of the treasures of poetry it contains, though treasures poured forth with indistinct profusion'; to Keats himself it seemed inexperienced and immature, and full of every error 'denoting a feverish attempt rather than a deed accomplished'. To write it was a compulsion he could not avoid; once it was written, he was content that it should be forgotten, while he prepared himself for what he called 'verses fit to live'. There was never a poet with fewer illusions.

The legend of Endymion is familiar to everybody, but it is pleasant to recall it in Keats's own words, because they were addressed to his little sister Fanny, then thirteen years old, and Keats's affection for her is one of the most endearing aspects of his character. He begins his letter – one of many – by telling Fanny, who was at school in Walthamstow, of his wish to become acquainted with all her little wants and enjoyments and urging her to write to him fully and frequently about whatever comes into her head. Then he mentions his poem, and goes on: 'Perhaps you might like to know what I am writing about. I will tell you. Many years ago there was a young handsome Shepherd who fed his flocks on a Mountain's Side called Latmus – he was a very contemplative sort of a Person and lived solitary amongst the Trees and Plains little thinking that such a beautiful Creature as the Moon was growing mad in Love with him. However so it was; and when he was asleep on the Grass she used to come down from heaven and admire him excessively for a long time; and at last could not refrain from carrying him away in her arms to the top of that high mountain Latmus while he was a-dreaming – but I dare say you have read this and all the other beautiful Tales which have come down from the ancient times of that beautiful Greece. If you have not, let me know and I will tell you more at large of others quite as delightful.'

While *Endymion* was being written and during the year that followed, Keats's chamber of maiden-thought was rapidly darkening, and he was beginning in earnest to explore the dark passages which led from it to another chamber more solemn and more magnificent. Two qualities which he possessed in a high degree, the gift for friendship which prompted him to be in constant communication by letter with the people he cared for, and the self-awareness which, in those letters, enabled him to reveal his innermost mind, have made him known to us with extraordinary completeness. With most men self-awareness is not very different from egotism, but it was not so with Keats; he never measured the world by himself, but always himself by the manner in which he responded to the ineluctable demands of living. That was his true greatness. The days of boyish enthusiasm with Hunt and his Hampstead friends were gone for ever. Hunt and Haydon and Reynolds were quarrelling, but Keats kept aloof; indeed, nobody could quarrel with Keats – his touch upon life was too sure. 'As soon as I had known Haydon three days,' he said, 'I got enough of his Character not to have been surprised at such a Letter as he has hurt you with'; and again: 'Men should bear with each other ... the best of men have but a portion of good in them, a kind of spiritual yeast in their frames, which creates the ferment of existence – by which a man is propelled to act, to strive, and buffet with Circumstance. The sure way is first to know a man's faults, and then be passive – if after that he insensibly draws you towards him, then you have no power to break the link.' The integrity of Keats's thinking is illustrated by the recurrence of certain key ideas in his poetry and letters at various stages in his life; one of these, his conception, gradually filled out and enriched, of a poet's growth to maturity, has already been mentioned; the insistence upon 'passivity' is another. Keats was not a theorist or systematic thinker; unlike Shelley, he never had a 'passion for reforming the world'; he never dreamed of looking upon himself as a teacher, as Wordsworth was too prone to do. He did, indeed, declare that he was ambitious of doing some good to the world, but it never for a moment occurred to him that he could do it by pointing out the world's errors. Was he not himself a part of the world, and were not its errors his own? For Keats, the business of a wise man was to live, not to invent a theory of life; to accept suffering, not to prescribe a patent medicine to avoid it; to go out in imaginative sympathy into the life of nature and of men, not to attempt to impose upon them an intellectual pattern. The mark, for Keats, of the true poet – and therefore of the highest human wisdom – was what he called 'negative capability' – when a man, that is, is 'capable of being in uncertainties, mysteries, doubts, without any irritable reaching after fact and reason'. Truth, in his view, could never be reached by consecutive reasoning – or, to put the same thing in other words – the intellect alone, being but one faculty amongst many, is necessarily a partial, and therefore an untrustworthy, guide. It is a view much more likely to be accepted nowadays than it was in Keats's time, and it is essentially a poet's view, because it implies the irrational element in all knowledge and the necessity of identification, as it were, of the perceiver with the perceived. 'When a sparrow comes before my window,' Keats wrote, 'I take part in its existence, and pick about the gravel.' To describe this immediate and intuitive grasp of the truth of things – or of the beauty of things, for beauty was, in Keats's belief, only another aspect of truth – he hit upon the word 'sensation' – and wrote the sentence which is most easy of all his sayings to misinterpret and which yet lies closer than any other to the heart of his thinking: 'Oh for a life of sensations rather than of thoughts!'

This fundamental mistrust of the intellect is in no way inconsistent with a wide learning. At the very moment that Keats was longing for a life of sensations rather than of thoughts, he was coming more and more to realize his ignorance. He was glad that he had not thrown away his medical books and determined to reread them to brush up his knowledge; he made plans to study Greek and Italian, and to get advice from Hazlitt upon a course of reading in metaphysics. 'An extensive knowledge', he wrote to Reynolds, 'is needful to thinking people – it takes away the heat and fever; and helps, by widening speculation, to ease the Burden of the Mystery, a thing which I begin to understand a little.' And then, with the instinct of a poet who sees all abstract ideas embodied in concrete images, he adds: 'The difference of high Sensations with and without knowledge appears to me this: in the latter case we are falling continually ten thousand fathoms deep and being blown up again, without wings, and with all the horror of a bare-shouldered creature – in the former case, our shoulders are fledged, and we go through the same air and space without fear.' Knowledge is power; but knowledge is not the product of the intellect alone – it is something deeper and more mysterious. It is not the scientist, as Matthew Arnold pointed out, who gives us the true sense of animals, or water, or plants – who 'makes us participate in their life' – but the poet. Shakespeare's daffodils which

> come before the swallow dares, and take
> The winds of march with beauty

are more 'real' for us than the daffodils in a botanist's handbook. Conscious as he was of his 'aching ignorance', Keats could still write in *What the Thrush said*:

> O fret not after knowledge; I have none,
> And yet my song comes native from the warmth.
> O fret not after knowledge; I have none,
> And yet the evening listens.

The two moods do not really contradict one another; they are complementary. The thrush knows what he needs to know, and therefore in his song there is no fretting and no regret.

By the beginning of 1818 Tom, the youngest brother, who had shown symptoms of consumption the previous year, was getting worse; his other brother, George, had decided to emigrate to America, and Keats's own health was not too good. The 'burden of the mystery' – that beautiful phrase which he was so fond of quoting from Wordsworth – was weighing upon him and his old exuberance of spirits was gone. 'I scarcely remember', he had already written, 'counting upon any happiness – I look not for it if it be not in the present hour'; and again, 'until we are sick we understand not; in fine, as Byron says, "Knowledge is sorrow"; and I go on to say that "Sorrow is wisdom" – and further for aught we can know with certainty "Wisdom is Folly".' They are heavy words for a young man of twenty-two, but there was no bitterness in them. Not long before, Keats had expressed the opinion that for a poet the best thing was a very gradual ripening of the intellectual powers; perhaps he was right, but in his own case the ripening had been extraordinarily swift, so that the experience of half a lifetime had been compressed into a couple of years. That, alone, brought its revenges; for all growth is painful, until the accession has been integrated and absorbed.

> It is a flaw [as Keats wrote],
> In happiness to see beyond our bourn;
> It forces us in summer skies to mourn;
> It spoils the singing of the nightingale.

In the March and April of this year Keats was with Tom at Teignmouth in Devonshire – that 'splashy rainy, misty, snowy, foggy, haily, floody, muddy, slipshod' county, as he called it: adding that the hills were very beautiful – when you get a sight of 'em. Tom's condition was a burden on Keats's heart – he was said to have been the nearest of the family to Keats himself in temperament – and all the time the thought of poetry, and perhaps the beginnings of doubt that he would be given the 'ten years' he had prayed for, were fermenting in his mind. His *Isabella* was written at this period, and his letters, chiefly those to Reynolds, are extraordinarily rich in those flashes of creative criticism, or inspired random commentary upon the nature and aim of poetry, which are peculiarly Keats's own. In all these comments what is perhaps most interesting is the beautiful consonance between Keats's view of poetry and his view of life: just as he mistrusted the attempt to impose an intellectual pattern upon dark and inscrutable mysteries, shunning dogma and creed, and preferring to lay himself open to life's secret influences as a plant lays itself open to sun and rain, so he mistrusted the poetry which, as he put it, 'has a palpable design upon us, and, if we do not agree, seems to put its hand into its breeches pocket.' Wordsworth, of course, was in his mind – Wordsworth, whom he once almost worshipped and still profoundly admired for what was best and truest in him, but whose peculiar weaknesses he now saw with an unerring eye. 'For the sake of a few fine imaginative or domestic passages, are we', he wrote, 'to be bullied into a certain Philosophy engendered in the whims of an Egotist?' 'Poetry' – again – 'should be great but unobtrusive, a thing which enters into one's soul'; and 'if poetry come not as naturally as leaves to a tree, it had better not come at all.'

Endymion was published in April of this year (1818), and it is characteristic of Keats that throughout the spring and the following summer he seems to have forgotten it. 'I never', he once declared, 'wrote a line of poetry with the least shadow of public thought', and he was one of the very few writers in the world for whom such a claim is justified. For Keats a poem once written was an old coat to be discarded; he was no longer concerned with it, but only with living its successor – as a tree might be supposed to forget the fallen blossom in the swelling of the fruit. By June Tom was much worse. Keats's mood was often deeply despondent, as if the darkness were closing in. 'I am never alone', he wrote to Reynolds, 'without rejoicing that there is such a thing as death – without placing my ultimate in the glory of dying for a great human purpose. Perhaps if my affairs were in a different state, I should not have written the above – you shall judge: I have two brothers; one is driven, by the "burden of Society", to America; the other with an exquisitive love of life, is in a lingering state. My love for my Brothers . . . has grown into an affection "passing the love of women". I have been ill-tempered with them – I have vexed them – but the thought of them has always stifled the impression that any woman might otherwise have made upon me. I have a sister too, and may not follow them either to America or the grave. Life must be undergone, and I certainly derive some consolation from the thought of writing one or two more poems before it ceases.' Perhaps he was right about the love of women – perhaps even Keats fell short, in this, of full self-knowledge. With Keats, however, despondency was not a negative thing; it was like slack-water at the change of tide, a period of waiting and expectancy. The 'one or two poems' were indeed to come, and they were to be made of the very stuff of his own deepest experience. The despondency, the sense that the flame was burning low before it blazed again, had already been described by Keats in the fourth book of *Endymion*, and indeed throughout his life it was a recurrent mood. The passage in *Endymion* is the well-known one about the Cave of Quietude, where

> Woe hurricanes beat ever at the gate,
> But all within is still and desolate;

a place of the spirit which all know, though few

> have ever felt how calm and well
> Sleep may be had in that deep den of all.

Sleep, indeed; but only as the prelude to an awakening, and an awakening, each time, to a richer and more beautiful, but more sombre, affirmation of life.

During the summer Keats arranged with his friend Charles Brown to go on a walking tour in Scotland, and George Keats having fixed his departure for America towards the end of June, the two companions decided to see him and his wife off at Liverpool, and to continue their tour from there. It was in the main a happy interlude for Keats, though it ended disastrously. Brown was a practical-minded, intelligent, somewhat coarse-grained young man, and an excellent companion for Keats, to whom he was devoted. For a time at any rate the change of habit and scene seems to have restored some of Keats's old physical exuberance, and as they climbed Skiddaw, 'I felt', he said, 'as if I were going to a Tournament', and he was planning in his mind to cover all Europe, later on, with his knapsack on his back. His letters, mostly to Tom and Fanny, were long, numerous, and amusing, packed with observation and shot with the little lambent flame of humour which was seldom extinguished even in his gravest moods. They are the very opposite of a sightseer's letters: they are intimate and casual talk to people he loved – the talk of a man with quick sympathies and an eye that missed nothing, an eye, moreover, which dwelt upon people and their ways with even more pleasure than upon the streams and mountains. 'Scenery is fine,' he had already written before he left Devonshire, 'but human nature is finer.' All true poets must come to that conclusion, and Keats more and more swiftly now was becoming attuned to

the still sad music of humanity;

yet not always either sad or still, as is shown by his description of the Scottish dancers who 'kickit and jumpit with mettle extraordinary, and whiskit and friskit, and toed it and go'd it, and twirl'd it and whirl'd it, and stamped it and sweated it, tattooing the floor like mad. The difference between our country dancers and these Scottish figures is about the same as leisurely stirring a cup o' Tea and beating up a batter-pudding.' Walking through Meg Merrilies' country, he puts into a letter for Fanny his lovely ballad about that old gipsy with her chip hat and red blanket cloak, and follows it by a string of nonsense verses about himself. At Burns's home, loving Burns he loathes the canting guide who professed to have known him: 'O the flummery of a birthplace!' he wrote. 'Cant! Cant! Cant! It is enough to give a spirit the guts-ache.'

They made a brief visit to Ireland, and then went as far

north as Inverness. Here Keats, whose throat had already been troubling him for some time, saw a doctor, who told him he must on no account return south on foot. Simultaneously news came from home of a sudden worsening of his brother Tom's condition. Keats, accordingly, parted from Brown and sailed from Cromarty in a smack for London. A friend described him on his arrival as being 'as brown and shabby as you can imagine; scarcely any shoes left, his jacket all torn at the back, a fur cap, a great plaid, and his knapsack.' The sore throat was the beginning of the end, and Keats, with his medical training, must have been perfectly aware that it was so.

A fortnight after his return a contemptuous and abusive article on *Endymion* appeared in Blackwood's *Edinburgh Magazine*. The vileness, virulence, and absurdity of the attack is difficult to understand in our better-mannered days. The motive was in part political: Blackwood's was a Tory magazine, and Keats was a friend of Hunt, who was a Liberal in politics and had already been subjected to similar treatment; partly, perhaps, it was a mere, cheap bid for notoriety. 'It is a better and a wiser thing', the writer declared, 'to be a starved apothecary than a starved poet, so back to the shop, Mr John, back to plasters, pills and ointment boxes etc. but for Heaven's sake, young Sangrado, be a little more sparing of extenuatives and soporifics in your practice than you have been in your poetry.' Lockhart – who was almost certainly in the main responsible for the article – was afterwards to be Scott's son-in-law and to write the great novelist's biography. He lived to be sorry for his abuse of Keats. Another review, in the *Quarterly*, was less insolent, but showed no more understanding of its subject than Lockhart did. Keats was bitterly hurt, as no sensitive person could fail to be; but the hurt was short-lived. Soon after, he was writing to his publisher a letter which is as interesting for the light it throws on the provenance of Keats's poetry as it is remarkable for its high courage. 'My own domestic criticism', he wrote, 'has given me pain without comparison beyond what Blackwood or the Quarterly could possibly inflict. . . . J.S. is perfectly right in regard to the slip-shod *Endymion*. That it is so is no fault of mine. No – though it may sound a little paradoxical. . . . Had I been nervous about its being a perfect piece, and with that view asked advice, and trembled over every page, it would not have been written; for it is not in my nature to fumble – I will write independently. I have written independently *without Judgement*. I may write independently, and *with Judgement*, hereafter. The Genius of Poetry must work out its own salvation in a man: it cannot be matured by law and precept, but by sensation and watchfulness in itself. . . . In *Endymion* I leapt headlong into the sea, and thereby have become better acquainted with the Soundings, the quicksands and the rocks, than if I had stayed upon the green shore, and piped a silly pipe, and took tea and comfortable advice. I was never afraid of failure.' And a few weeks later he says to his brother George, 'This is a mere matter of the moment: I think I shall be among the English Poets after my death.' A man's life is not subject – happily – to mathematical analysis; but these letters are enough to prove that the story, which both Byron and Shelley helped to perpetuate, that Keats was killed by adverse and anonymous criticism – the 'shaft that flies in darkness' – is very far from the truth. Like most great artists, he had fibres in his being much too tough for that.

Meanwhile he was watching by the bedside of his dying brother. He nursed him for three months, 'obliged', as he put it, 'to write and plunge into abstract images to ease myself of his countenance, his voice, and feebleness – so that I live now in a continual fever'. The poetry, though necessary to him, seemed a kind of disloyalty to Tom; but it was not to be denied, and at the same time another longing began to make itself felt: 'I was never in love,' he wrote to Reynolds, 'yet the voice and shape of a Woman has haunted me these two days. . . . This morning poetry has conquered – I feel escaped from a new, strange, and threatening sorrow, and I am thankful for it. There is an awful warmth about my heart, like a load of immortality.' He was twenty-three, and by nature passionate – he himself spoke of the violence of his temperament 'continually smothered down'; the very presence of death, as he watched by the sick-bed, accentuated his longing for love. But he was at the same time afraid of it, and of what it might do to him if it came. In his letters to America he protests his determination never to marry; the generality of women, he says, appear to him as children to whom he would rather give a sugar-plum than his time – yet all the while he knows that he has not really escaped from the new, strange, and threatening sorrow. Nor had he; exactly when, we do not know, but some time before Tom's death he met Fanny Brawne. No man ever foresaw the future in the instant with a more fatal clarity than Keats.

It is difficult to be just to Fanny Brawne. She was eighteen when she met Keats, and full of high spirits, vivacity, and charm. Keats's first mention of her in a letter is disparaging – possibly self-defensive: 'Mrs Brawne', he writes, 'is a very nice woman, and her daughter senior is I think beautiful and elegant, graceful, silly, fashionable and strange – we have a little tiff now and then, and she behaves better, or I must have sheered off.' Then he calls her 'monstrous in behaviour, flying out in all directions, calling people such names that I was forced lately to make use of the term *Minx* – this is, I think, not from any innate vice but from a penchant she has for acting stylishly.' Within a week, however, of their first meeting, Keats had passed into her absolute dominion, and, with his surrender, had entered upon the two years of tormented love and jealousy which were to hasten the course of his disease, and kill him. There seems to be no doubt that Fanny Brawne was fond of him; but to answer the demands which a man of Keats's temperament could not but make, called for something of a heroic quality which Fanny did not possess.

The poem which Keats began by Tom's bedside was *Hyperion*. Immediately after Tom's death, which occurred on 1 December 1818, Keats left his lodging in Well Walk, Hampstead, and went to live with Brown at Wentworth Place, next door to other mutual friends, the Dilkes. The future was dark for him: his brother (and best friend) George was on the other side of the world; Tom was dead; the beginnings of consumption had already declared themselves; he had been publicly insulted by the reviews; his money affairs were in poor order and he had little hope of earning anything by his pen; and now, on the top of all this, there was the anguish of a love which could not possibly be fulfilled. It was in these circumstances that the period of his greatest poetry began. The matter and manner of this poetry is the measure of his response to the challenge of misfortune. Two of the poems, the *Eve of St Agnes* and the *Ode to Psyche*, are happy poems, warm from the moments of exaltation and imagined enjoyment of love, which were undoubtedly his; the others, in particular the two versions of *Hyperion*, tell of a triumph, indeed, but a triumph of a wholly different kind. Not long before, Keats had referred to 'the mighty abstract Idea', which he had, 'of Beauty in all things'; he was to repeat the phrase later in almost the same words to Fanny Brawne, and at Teignmouth in the spring of 1818 he had written in a verse-letter to Reynolds the words:

> O never will the prize
> High reason, and the love of good and ill,
> Be my award.

These phrases – 'beauty in all things', and the 'love of good and ill' – are of vital importance, if the pattern of Keats's life is to be understood. Both of them suggest – what is, of course, fully embodied in the greatest of his poetry – the nature of the final stage in the growth of a poet, as Keats conceived it, and at which he had himself arrived. It is a condition beyond both sorrow and joy; the realization that only the truth – only reality – which by the very ordering of human life is destructive of individual happiness – is beautiful. It is submission, not in despair but in thankfulness, to the necessity of life and death. Only the poet, like the Titan Oceanus in *Hyperion*, can say to those who have been defeated by life's inexorable processes, and are yet themselves a part of those processes,

> Receive the truth, and let it be your balm.

The last of his great odes was the *Ode to Autumn*. Keats never wrote a more tranquil poem; the slow-moving words, known to every lover of English poetry, are heavy-laden with harvest:

> Where are the songs of Spring? Ay, where are they?
> Think not of them, thou hast thy music too –

It is a deeper and nobler music, though the day is dying, and the year is dying, and the swallows are gathering to follow the departing sun.

Early in 1819, probably in January, Keats became engaged to Fanny Brawne. He did not speak of his engagement to his friends, or even mention it in his letters to George in America. It was the one subject upon which he was dumb. Were it not for a few recorded words of his spoken to Severn shortly before his death, and one letter to Brown from Naples, we should know nothing of the course of his love except from the letters he wrote to Fanny Brawne herself. Many of these have been preserved, and most of them are too painful to read. He was in great distress for money; the legacy from his grandfather could not be touched until his sister Fanny came of age, yet even so he lent Haydon a sum which he could ill spare. For a time it seemed as if, despite his failing health, he would have to give up poetry and find some regular employment, and he seriously considered going to sea as surgeon in an East Indiaman. Jealousy of his lighthearted lover was rapidly becoming an unendurable anguish, but he could still find time to write to his sister letters full of affection and brotherly concern, and even of gaiety; and there was a flash of his old boyhood's pugnacity and zest, when he met a butcher teasing a kitten, and fought him with his fists for an hour, and beat him.

Brown was strongly opposed to the idea of Keats going to sea, and persuaded him instead to accept an advance of money and to collaborate in writing a play for the stage. Keats consented, and went to Shanklin in the Isle of Wight, where Brown soon afterwards joined him. The play, *Otho the Great*, was written, but came to nothing, as the actor Kean, for whom it was designed, left England. For a time after that Keats was in Winchester, where he wrote his *Lamia*; but still there were no prospects of his earning a living, and he had thoughts of turning his hand to journalism. From June to October of this year he did not see Fanny Brawne – he did not dare. In October, however, his resolution broke, and he went to Wentworth Place – the other half of Brown's house, where she was living. From that moment any strength he had acquired to withstand his misery was gone. In the final months of the year he began his last work; the remodelled version of *Hyperion*, a poem which, though it contains passages finer than any others he had written, shows some signs of failing power. On 3 February 1820, he came home to Hampstead in a high fever. Brown put him at once to bed. He coughed slightly – and there was blood on the pillow. Quite calmly he looked up at his friend, and said: 'I know the colour of that blood – it is arterial blood. That drop of blood is my death-warrant. I must die.'

A few months before, in the second version of his *Hyperion*, he had described in memorable words the ultimate vision of the poet – the vision of life seen in final calm beyond the reach of joy or sorrow. The image by which he suggests it is the face of the goddess Moneta, who lifts her veils before his eyes:

> Then saw I a wan face,
> Not pined by human sorrows, but bright-blanch'd
> By an immortal sickness which kills not;
> It works a constant change, which happy death
> Can put no end to; deathwards progressing
> To no death was that visage; it had past
> The lily and the snow; and beyond these
> I must not think now, though I saw that face.
> But for her eyes I should have fled away;
> They held me back with a benignant light,
> Soft-mitigated by divinest lids
> Half-closed, and visionless entire they seemed
> Of all external things: they saw me not,
> But in blank splendour beamed like the mild moon,
> Who comforts those she sees not, who knows not
> What eyes are upward cast.

Keats had had his vision, and his triumph. But now his body was broken, and perhaps his heart. He lived nearly a year longer – a sort of posthumous existence.

He and Fanny Brawne were now next-door neighbours. He saw her constantly, but her presence, or nearness, were a torment to him. Friends visited him, and from time to time he seemed a little better, and was able to go out. But the progress of the disease was nevertheless inexorable. In July Shelley, with the generosity which was characteristic of him, invited him to join him in Italy – and to teach him Greek. But Keats refused. In the same month his last volume of poems was published – the volume which put him (in the words he had once used) 'amongst the English poets'. The first review of it was Charles Lamb's, and full of warm and discriminating praise. The *Edinburgh* praised him too. But the praise had come too late; and Keats was past caring for it. Then the doctors told him that his only hope – a slender one – was to winter out of England, and Keats, too weary, perhaps, to oppose, or perhaps in dread of what he knew would be a last good-bye to his lover, consented to go. On September 17th with his friend Severn he embarked at the London docks on the brig *Maria Crowther*, bound for Naples, which was reached thirty-four days later. After being released from quarantine he wrote to Brown, unable to disguise his misery: 'O God, God, God! Everything I have in my trunks that reminds me of her goes through me like a spear. . . . I am afraid to write to her – to receive a letter from her – to see her handwriting would break my heart. . . . My dear Brown, what am I to do?' Early in November the two friends moved to Rome, and for a few days a little flame of life flickered up again in the sick man. Severn played to him on the piano; he even went out riding, and meditated a new poem. 'If I recover,' he wrote again to Brown, 'I will do all in my power to correct the mistakes made during sickness; and if I should not, all my faults will be forgiven.' His sister Fanny was much in his thoughts – 'walking about his imagination like a ghost'. 'I can scarcely bid you good-bye,' he wrote, 'even in a letter. I always make an awkward bow.' Early in December, however, the hope of improvement was finally dashed. On successive days he had violent haemorrhages and high fever. Severn nursed him with the tenderness of a woman, for two months never leaving him, reading to him by day and night, cooking for him, making his bed, and sweeping the room. Sometimes he would play Haydn sonatas to him on the piano, and Keats took pleasure in the music. He would invent little tricks and devices to distract the attention of the dying man from his misery; he has told us how in watching Keats he would sometimes fall asleep, and, when he awoke, find that they were in the dark. 'To remedy this one night,' he wrote, 'I tried the experiment of fixing a thread from the bottom of a lighted candle to the wick of an unlighted one, that the flame might be conducted, all which I did without telling Keats. When he awoke and found the first candle nearly out, he was reluctant to wake me, and while doubting suddenly cried out, "Severn, Severn, here's a little fairy lamplighter actually lit up the other candle".' Severn was the one solid rock to which he clung: 'Poor Keats has me ever by him, and shadows out the form of one solitary friend: he opens his eyes in great doubt and horror, and when they fall on me they close gently, open quietly and close again, till he sinks to sleep.'

As death approached, Keats grew calmer. He allowed himself to be drawn by Severn to some of the comforts of religion, and would listen quietly while his friend read passages from Jeremy Taylor's *Holy Living and Holy Dying*. When the doctor visited him, 'Doctor,' was his habitual question, 'when will this posthumous life of mine come to an end?' – and it seems to have been without any bitterness that he suggested for his epitaph the words: 'Here lies one whose name was writ in water.'

His last words were in consideration for his friend: 'Severn – lift me up – I am dying – I shall die easy. Don't be frightened – be firm, and thank God it has come.' He died on 23 February 1821, and three days later he was buried in the English Cemetery in Rome, where within eighteen months his body was to be joined by Shelley's.

Churchill

WINSTON SPENCER CHURCHILL, grandson of the seventh Duke of Marlborough, was born at Blenheim Palace on 30 November 1874. His father was Lord Randolph Churchill and his mother – before her marriage Miss Jeannette Jerome – was the daughter of an American business man and newspaper proprietor. It was a romantic marriage. Both were young – Lord Randolph twenty-four, Jennie Jerome nineteen and beautiful. They met in August during Cowes Week, and three days later, finding themselves together after dinner on a beautiful night, warm and still, with the lights of the yachts shining in the water and the sky bright with stars, Lord Randolph proposed and was accepted. As in those far off days an eyebrow was apt to be lifted at the prospect of a duke's son marrying the daughter of an American man of business, there were family objections to the engagement; but they were overcome, and the marriage took place in the following April. Human nature is unpredictable, and the habit, dear to biographers, of explaining a man's character by his origins, is more amusing than profitable; nevertheless, this triumph of young blood and determined departure from the ducal norm seem a fitting background for a life like Sir Winston Churchill's, a life which owes less to convention and more to the clamant and imperious zest for experience than that of any statesman of modern times.

Of his mother, Sir Winston Churchill has written: 'She shone for me like the evening star, I loved her dearly but at a distance. She always seemed to me a fairy princess'; his father, who had himself a brief but brilliant political career, he loved, and deeply admired, but at a greater distance still; for during his childhood they were kept apart by the nursery, that once powerful but now almost forgotten stronghold of the English home; and then came school, and then the army, and in 1895, when Sir Winston was twenty-one, Lord Randolph died. 'All my dreams', Sir Winston Churchill wrote, 'of comradeship with him, of entering Parliament at his side and in his support were ended. There remained for me only to pursue his aims and vindicate his memory.'

Yet the nursery did not entirely separate father and son; for it is said that on one occasion Lord Randolph, upon entering it, found the boy playing with his lead soldiers, a large army which he loved with passion, and asked him if he would like, one day, to be a soldier himself. The answer was an unhesitating 'Yes'. It was not originally intended that Winston Churchill should enter the Army, but it had begun to be clear to his parents that his abilities were not of the kind that would succeed in the profession of law. Indeed, they were barely adequate, as soon afterwards appeared, to get him into Harrow. No one, of course, with any knowledge of children will be surprised at this: it is the academic intelligence which declares itself early and flatters the self-esteem of the preparatory school masters, whose task is to nurture it; but minds of a strong original bent are wont to abide their time.

Sir Winston did not like Harrow much, though in later life he has been very kind to his old school. He found the Classics pointless and boring, and (as no polo was played) he did not care for the games. But he enjoyed reading, and already wrote with enough ease and fluency to make it worth his while to do a little trade in kind – one English essay for one Latin translation; and he delighted in fencing, leaving Harrow with the Public Schools fencing championship. Sandhurst he failed to enter at the first two attempts, but succeeded at the third, after working with an army crammer. Before this, however, he made his first acquaintance with the world of politics – at his father's side, but not, unhappily, for lon 5. An accident (he had fallen off a tree) kept him in London to convalesce, and here he was enabled to meet many of the leading political figures of the day, his father's friends, and to listen from the gallery of the House of Commons to Gladstone, then in his eighty-fifth year, speaking for Irish Home Rule. This was the time when the young Mr Churchill longed to enter Parliament and share his father's battles; but Lord Randolph already knew that his career was over, and two years later he was dead. Meanwhile, Sir Winston had been admitted to Sandhurst and found himself a cavalry cadet. It was a happy change from Harrow, for the work to be done, unlike the Classics, had evidently some bearing upon practical affairs and the doings of men. Nine-tenths of distinguished Englishmen have looked back upon their Public Schools, which are the most English of all English institutions, at best with a mildly contemptuous, though affectionate, tolerance, and at the worst with strong distaste. Sir Winston Churchill is no exception.

At the age of twenty he was gazetted to the Fourth Hussars, commanded by Colonel Brabazon, an accomplished soldier with a fine record of service. It was a period when England was on top of the world. The great Victorian age was drawing to its close, and for the majority of well-to-do Englishmen the future seemed to shine with undiminished lustre. Under the surface, ideas were moving and disruptive forces were at work, as indeed they are at every moment of history, to the discomfiture of the rapid and impressionistic historian: socialism was already raising its head: the ignominy and shame of poverty in the midst of wealth had long since been portrayed by novelists. Science since the appearance of the *Origin of Species* had been waging for more than thirty years its fierce but phantasmal battle with religion, and one poet at least, grieving that the tide of faith was on the ebb, had heard only

the melancholy, long, withdrawing roar

of the breakers along the naked shingles of the world. Odd things were happening in art and literature: Beardsley was drawing pictures that the old Queen would not approve, Wilde had just written his *Salomé*, and the young Bernard Shaw was getting into trouble with the censor over *Mrs Warren's Profession* and beginning to stand upon his head in the attitude which, according to Sir Max Beerbohm, he never afterwards abandoned. None of these things, however, was likely to trouble a young cavalry subaltern in the Fourth Hussars, freed at last from the tutelage of school and Sandhurst and moving happily amongst men. For him, as for the majority of his countrymen, they were only the surface glitter and froth on the untroubled depths of the great English certainties; Germany and Russia might have their imperial ambitions, but England was supreme upon the oceans of the world and need have no fear; England's peculiar brand of democracy, tough yet flexible like any other growing and healthy organism, would last for ever; England's ever-increasing wealth and material prosperity; her decency and honour; her sense of the rightness and inevitability of her great station and confidence in divine sanction for her commercial enterprise; the soundness of conscience which was ready to accept Kipling's reminder that it was only under the awful hand of the Lord God of Hosts that she held, and would continue to hold, 'dominion over palm and pine': all this was much more instant and engaging than the antics of a few *fin de siècle* intellectuals, the premonitory rumblings of social discontent, or even the stirrings of ambition in continental powers.

Hearts beat high at twenty, and it is not surprising therefore that Lieutenant Churchill, rejoicing as he did in the jingle of harness, the stir of the horses, the colour and gallant movement, the pageantry and sense of comradeship and shared purpose, found with his regiment a 'gay and lordly life'. The purpose, indeed, was there; but it was not, at the moment, very insistent or conspicuous; a fighting force is intended to fight, but it was already forty years since the Crimea, the last occasion on which England had gone to war with a civilized country, and it seemed very unlikely that she would go to war again, except for small punitive or precautionary campaigns against savages in some outpost of Empire. Not even one of these actually offered itself in 1895; but Lieutenant Churchill was determined, being a soldier, to do a soldier's job: somewhere or other he must find a war. He found it in Cuba, where, in a modest way, the Cuban patriots were defying the Spaniards. Through the influence of the British Ambassador in Madrid he succeeded in getting himself attached to a flying column in the Spanish army, and, on his twenty-first birthday, heard shots fired in anger for the first time. It was a poor little war, but the best to be had at the moment, and Lieutenant Churchill found it an exhilarating experience. He had seen the bright eyes of danger, and loved them, as he has loved them ever since.

Back in England, he found his regiment under orders for India. At Bangalore time hung heavy on his hands, for it was no longer enough that life should be gay and lordly; it must also be active, and polo and parades failed to satisfy his eager and restless spirit. So he turned to reading. He read with zest and extreme rapidity – he shares with Dr Johnson the happy faculty of getting the meat out of a book at a single swallow, and promptly digesting it. He began with Gibbon, his father's favourite, went on to more history, and then to philosophy, delighting in new worlds of intellectual experience which school had failed to reveal. Home on leave again, he heard the news that trouble had broken out on the North-West frontier, and at once decided that he must not miss it. His own regiment was not to be actively employed, but the commanding officer on the spot, Sir Bindon Blood, was a friend of his, and might manage something. Lieutenant Churchill sent a telegram. The answer was satisfactory, and he left for India without delay. On the way, at Brindisi, he learnt that his only chance of serving depended upon his being employed, in addition, as a war correspondent. The check was momentary: the *Pioneer* of Allahabad offered to print his dispatches, and Lady Randolph – to the end of her life his devoted accomplice – persuaded the London *Telegraph* to do the same. The next thing was to get leave from his regiment, still stationed at Bangalore. It was done in a rush – south, and then north again, a journey of two thousand miles, until he found himself at the headquarters of the Malakand Field Force on the frontier. This was a better war than the Cuban, and in consequence more keenly enjoyed. Lieutenant Churchill was mentioned in dispatches for 'making himself useful at a critical moment'. The moment he has himself described with gusto and humour: a Pathan warrior had slashed with his sword at the body of the fallen adjutant, when (Sir Winston writes) 'I forgot everything else except a desire to kill this man. I wore my long cavalry sword well sharpened. After all, I had won the Public Schools Fencing Medal. I resolved on personal combat à l'arme blanche. The savage saw me coming ... he picked up a big stone and hurled it at me with his left hand, and then awaited me, brandishing his sword. There were others waiting not far behind.

'I changed my mind about the cold steel. I pulled out my revolver, took, as I thought, most careful aim, and fired. No result. I fired again. No result. I fired again. Whether I hit him or not I cannot tell. At any rate, he ran back two or three yards and plumped down behind a rock.'

By this time Churchill was alone; all around, musketry fire was heavy and continuous. He made off as fast as he could to where he thought his friends were concealed, and found them, thankfully, behind a knoll. A few days later he was posted to the 31st Punjaub Infantry and soon won the confidence of his men, and loved them as they loved him – though he could speak to them but three words: the Hindustani for 'get on' and 'kill', and the useful English word 'tally-ho'. This campaign in the Mahmund Valley was afterwards extended and assumed more serious proportions, but Churchill's leave was up, and though he made every effort to continue on active service, he was forced to rejoin his regiment at Bangalore. Once more polo and parades left ample leisure, and this time he filled it not by reading only but by writing. His newspaper articles had been well received, so he decided to expand them into a book, and the result was his first published volume – it appeared in 1898 – *The Story of the Malakand Field Force*.

The book was a success. It was praised in the Press, and read by the Prime Minister and the Prince of Wales. One reason, no doubt, for its popularity was the novel spectacle it afforded of an army subaltern sitting in judgement on his superior officers. The subaltern enjoyed doing it as much as the public enjoyed seeing it done; but his criticism of the conduct of the campaign was also for him a serious matter, for Sir Winston, in his youth, not only found danger exhilarating, but understood the strategy of war. He has, it seems, always understood it, even in the nursery; but live soldiers are better than lead ones. The book had been easily and swiftly written – Churchill is almost as rapid a writer as reader: he followed the *Malakand Field Force* with a novel which he completed in eight weeks – and it brought its author a good deal more money than his subaltern's pay. This fact may have started in his mind the idea that, though a soldier's life was fun, he might not wish to remain a soldier for ever. Meanwhile, however, more campaigns were on the way, in a rising scale of gay adventure. In the summer of 1898 Kitchener, Sirdar of the Egyptian Army, was on the march against the Mahdi's heir in the Sudan to avenge the death of Gordon. Churchill lost no time in applying for attachment to Kitchener's force. Kitchener himself refused three urgent requests – one of them sent through no less a person than Lord Salisbury, the Prime Minister, who had asked to meet the young author of the *Malakand Field Force*. Three firm refusals from the Commander-in-Chief might have deterred other men; it did not deter Churchill. With Lady Randolph's help he persuaded the Adjutant-General, Sir Evelyn Wood, to attach him to the 21st Lancers, with orders to report in Cairo at once, and under condition that he received no pay while on service and brought no charge upon army funds in the event of being killed or wounded. The loss of pay was more than compensated by a commission from the *Morning Post* to print his letters from the front.

The 21st Lancers joined the army just before the final battle at Omdurman. On the morning of the battle it fell to Churchill himself to report the approach of the enemy to the Commander-in-Chief. 'Talk of fun,' he wrote years later; 'where will you beat this! On horseback, at daybreak, within shot of an advancing army, seeing everything, and corresponding direct with Head-quarters.' Before many hours were gone, the Mahdist army had been shattered by the musketry fire of the

British and Egyptians, but there was still work left for the 21st Lancers. Ordered to clear the ground, they wheeled into line for the charge, three hundred against three thousand. It was a costly gesture; though the enemy line was broken, and the Dervishes fell back, the Lancers lost a quarter of their strength. Churchill's first words, when the charge was over, were 'Did you enjoy it?' The sergeant whom he addressed, a sensible man, indicated by his reply that he could fancy more agreeable ways of spending his time; but not so Lieutenant Churchill: for him those three breathless minutes had been bliss. Never had the eyes of danger shone so bright, never had life tasted so sharp upon his tongue.

Immediately after Omdurman he sailed for home. Already a successful journalist and author and with material for a second book ready to hand, he decided to rejoin his regiment in India for the last time and to send in his papers the following year. He would make a living by his pen, relieve Lady Randolph of the burden of his allowance, and enter Parliament. In 1899, therefore, he was a civilian again, and deeply engaged upon his *River War*, a long survey of the rise and fall of Mahdism and the reconquest of the Sudan. The book was an advance upon his first, and firmly established his reputation as a writer upon military matters. It was notable for the strong criticism it contained of certain aspects of Kitchener's command, in particular of his desecration of the Mahdi's tomb. It is always the gay fighter who is the chivalrous one.

Now, for the first time, he turned his attention seriously to politics. In spite of his inability to contribute to party funds, he was adopted as a Tory candidate for the two-member constituency of Oldham. In politics as in war he soon revealed his disconcerting habit of thinking for himself, opposing, during the election campaign, the Government's Tithes Bill, and thereby earned a rebuke from Mr Balfour, who at that time led the Conservatives in the House of Commons. Churchill was not elected, but something even more valuable to his future career happened instead – a glare of publicity in the *Daily Mail*, where his friend G. W. Steevens, the distinguished war correspondent, wrote him up as the Youngest Man in Europe, with 'qualities which make him, almost at will, a great popular leader, a great journalist, or the founder of a great advertising business'. This was even more gratifying than the comment of Mr Walter Runciman, the successful Liberal candidate, after the result of the contest had been declared: 'I don't think,' he said to his unsuccessful rival, 'that the world has seen the last of either of us.'

Only a few of the countless Englishmen to whom Sir Winston Churchill's physical presence is today as familiar as their next-door neighbour's can remember him as a young man. It is worth while, therefore, to recall a description of him by an acute and sympathetic observer, Wilfrid Scawen Blunt, who made his acquaintance in 1903: 'He is a little square-headed fellow of no very striking appearance, but of wit, intelligence and originality. In mind and manner he is a strange replica of his father, with all his father's suddenness and assurance, and I should say more than his father's ability. There is just the same *gaminerie* and contempt of the conventional and the same engaging plain spokenness and readiness to understand.' The words sound oddly now that Sir Winston Churchill is the most justly celebrated figure of modern times; but they are subtly perceptive, and lay a finger upon most of the qualities which have made him both eminent and beloved.

Some might say that Winston Churchill in his youth was a lucky man; but most of what one calls luck is a compound of character and circumstance. Up to 1899, in spite of the prophetic article in the *Daily Mail*,

Churchill was in no sense a public figure; but with the coming of the Boer War he leapt into prominence and caught for the first time the imagination of the British people. He sailed for South Africa as special correspondent of the *Morning Post*, was at once involved in the thick of the fighting, in which, though a civilian, he played a vigorous and characteristic part, and was taken prisoner. No sooner was he shut up in Pretoria than he began to plan his escape. The chance soon came. He slipped out, alone, climbed a wall while the sentries' backs were turned, and, with nothing in his pocket but a little money and a few slabs of chocolate, set off on the three hundred mile walk to Delagoa Bay. Soon it occurred to him that it would be better to travel by rail, so he boarded a moving east-bound train, travelled throughout the night, and slipped off again just before daybreak. The Boers had put a price on his head; hiding till dark, he struggled on, and fell in with a British colliery owner, who concealed him for some days in a mine shaft. Then, packing himself on another train amongst some bales of wool, he reached the frontier in safety. After that he returned to the scene of the fighting, got a commission in the South African Light Horse, and was present at the relief of Ladysmith and the march to Johannesburg and Pretoria. It was a grand prelude to a parliamentary career. On his return, half England 'loved him for the perils he had passed', like Desdemona when she heard Othello's story; for fifty years ago England was more innocent than she is today, and had not yet supped full with horrors or heard so many tales of wild adventure and heroism as to take them as a matter of course. Sir Winston Churchill's Boer War had, on the surface, just the quality of insouciance and gay adventure that his countrymen found irresistible – or half of them, for England was divided over the war, and one section had been strongly opposed to it from the beginning. Churchill himself had learnt much; he had been impressed by the beastliness as well as the brilliance of warfare; his view that seniority is not the best proof of an officer's competence had been powerfully confirmed, and it was typical of him that he was amongst the first to express an opinion upon the fine fighting qualities and patriotic virtues of the Boers, and to recommend a generous and forgiving policy when the war was over.

In the autumn of 1900 he was elected as junior member for Oldham, and employed the interval before the new Parliament met by lecturing in England and America on his adventures. When Parliament did meet early in the following year, Queen Victoria was dead and Edward VII was on the throne.

It is not possible here to follow in detail Sir Winston's half-century of political activity; it will be best to consider it merely as the background to the superb service which he rendered to his country during the war against Nazi Germany. He has never been a good 'party man'; his enemies have called him an opportunist, and one observer, by no means an enemy, wrote of him in 1907 as 'convinced of ability to dominate Army, Navy, and either political party, though naturally uncertain which' – in fact, as Wilfrid Blunt had already remarked, sudden and assured. From the first moment of his entry into Parliament as Conservative member for Oldham, he was an uncomfortable colleague, for he was already in many respects a Liberal at heart, as possibly he has remained ever since – if Liberalism means an open mind and ordered progress within the framework of society as we know it. British troops were still in South Africa, but Churchill was paying tributes in the House to the chivalry and patriotism of the Boers, much to the embarrassment of Chamberlain and the party leaders; soon he was to attack the Secretary of State for War upon the Army estimates; and finally Chamberlain's campaign for protection made his position as a convinced free-trader untenable. His father, Lord Randolph, had rebelled against Tory policy, but party loyalty had kept him from changing sides – and ruined him. The son, on the contrary, refused to be bound; preferring, like Brutus, to

> take the current when it served
> Or lose his ventures,

he crossed the floor of the House and took his seat with the Liberals. Liberalism in 1905 was a rising force, and it was already clear that Balfour's government was done for. Before the end of the year it was out, and Churchill took office under Campbell-Bannerman as Under-Secretary for the Colonies. This same year his biography of Lord Randolph appeared: he had written it mainly at the House of Commons, in the intervals of his work there. The book – the best of his books with the possible exception of his *Second World War* – fulfilled the promise to vindicate his father's memory.

As Under-Secretary for the Colonies Sir Winston's chief concern was the settlement in South Africa, and his first-hand knowledge of the country and its people gave him an advantage in debate over most other members of the House, and his policy and that of the Liberal Government which he served was justified in 1914 and 1939, when the Union of South Africa rallied to the Crown. He also found time to visit Germany to watch the Army manoeuvres, during which he had talk with the Kaiser, who already seemed to think him a young man of sufficient importance to notice. By 1908 King Edward was speaking of him in flattering terms, and when, on the retirement of Campbell-Bannerman, Asquith succeeded to the Premiership, Churchill was included in the new Cabinet as President of the Board of Trade. Thus, at the age of thirty-three, he found himself a member of the most brilliant Cabinet of modern times, the colleague of Asquith, Haldane, Grey, Lloyd George, and the old philosopher and man of letters, John Morley, the affectionate friend who was to praise his 'vitality, his indefatigable industry and attention to business, his remarkable gift of language and skill in argument, and his curious flair for all sorts of political cases as they arise'. In September of this year he married Miss Clementine Hozier, and, as he was to write twenty-two years later, 'lived happily ever afterwards'. The family was to be united by the strongest ties, and he was as fortunate as a husband as he had been as a son. Asked once if his infant daughter was a pretty child, 'The prettiest in the world,' he replied. 'Like her mother, I suppose?' 'No,' said Sir Winston gravely; 'she is exactly like me.'

He had by now become a close friend of Lloyd George and the friendship helped to develop the Radical element in his political sympathies. The condition of the poor – who he declared were worse off in England than anywhere, even in the East – began more and more to occupy his attention. 'I would give my life', he once said, 'to see them placed on a right footing in regard to their lives and means of living. That is what I am paid for, and I would really give my life.' He vigorously supported Lloyd George's budget proposals – the revolutionary budget (as it then seemed), designed to pay for the new social services, and the Bill against the veto of the Lords, whom he gaily caricatured in Parliament as 'revolving the problems of Empire and of Epsom'. His friend Blunt has recorded that though he was a professed Imperialist, Churchill was in general sympathy with his ideas about the enslavement of coloured peoples by the whites, even going so far as to confide to his diary the hope that he would one day come round to the view that the British should withdraw from India. As Home Secretary (which he became in 1910) he threw himself into the scheme of prison reform. To prisoners, as to the poor, his feelings were humane and generous, and the burden of deciding appeals against capital sentences weighed upon his mind. Seeing a performance of Galsworthy's *Justice*, he was so deeply moved that he abolished solitary confinement. Once a certain financier was convicted of embezzlement and sent to prison. Admiral Sir Randolph Foote, who knew the man, was convinced that his crime was due more to muddle-headedness than knavery, and wrote to the Home Secretary, asking for clemency and promising to go bail for the prisoner's future good behaviour. The sentence was duly shortened, and several years afterwards Churchill, then First Lord of the Admiralty, happened to be inspecting some naval guns in a coastal battery of which Admiral Foote was in charge. Sir Winston recognized the Admiral, and said: 'That chap you made me let out – did he go straight?' 'Yes.' 'I thought he would,' was Sir Winston's answer. Even today, forty years later, his name is still a name to conjure with in prisons. When Dingra, the Indian patriot and fanatic, was hanged for political murder, Churchill, though he approved the necessity of the sentence, admired the man. Dingra's last words, a selfless declaration of faith in his impossible cause, Churchill declared were the finest expression of patriotism ever heard, and would be remembered as long as Regulus and Plutarch's heroes. For Irish Home Rule he fought hard and long, saying on one occasion to John Redmond that his life's ambition was to bring in a Home Rule Bill as Chief Secretary, and Redmond believed him. He was rapidly becoming, with Lloyd George, joint leader of the advanced Liberals in the House of Commons, and speculation was already beginning as to which of the two would become Prime Minister first. 'But what is the use', Lloyd George said, 'of being jealous of Winston?' His Radicalism made him bitter enemies amongst

the Tories, his old party. The obvious charge against
him was that of being a turncoat and deserter – a crime
infinitely aggravated by his subsequent success. It was
a foolish accusation, though, doubtless, natural enough.
He was to turn his coat again later – if the phrase must
be used; but the fact is that there may be a greater betrayal
of principle in refusing to desert a political party than in
deserting it. Political principles are one thing, political
expedients another, and it would not be difficult to show
that the former have remained, in general, pretty constant throughout Sir Winston Churchill's long parliamentary career. The chief of them have been a passionate
love, based on a typically English blend of realism and
romance, of England and her imperial destiny, a hatred
of oppression and tyranny between nations or between
classes within the nation, and fear of Socialism as the
destroyer of individual liberty. Power he loved for its
own sake, and looked forward to it from his first entry
into politics – 'I feel', he once said, 'as if I could lift the
universe on my shoulders'; it was a part of the invincible
vitality, which his friend Morley remarked in him, and
of his incomparable zest for the game of politics, and
for the game of life. Indeed, everyone who has been in
contact with him has remarked the same – the boundless
gusto for the mere fact of living, which in spite of his
ceaseless concern with contemporary problems seems
to make him a revenant from a younger world. It was
this buoyancy of spirit which made 'fun' for him of the
cavalry charge at Omdurman, and it is the same quality
which has made of his life a refutation of Lord Acton's
familiar saying, 'power corrupts'. Power never corrupted
Sir Winston Churchill, for the simple reason that he has
had no need to suck his sense of life from others' submission, but possesses it within himself in sufficient
abundance. This is the fundamental basis of Churchill's
character – as it is, perhaps, the fundamental basis of

the British character as a whole. The buds and blossoms which have grown from this root have been, in the course of Sir Winston's career, of astonishing variety and vividness; the same zest for experience and sense of the sheer richness and delightfulness of living which made him enjoy, as a young man, the adventure of war (it is only those who fear life who are afraid of death), have made him enjoy all sorts of other things very far removed from the beaten track of public life: painting, for instance (about which he has written one of the pleasantest of his books), and bricklaying (he joined the Amalgamated Union of Building Trade Workers as an adult apprentice); clothes of an idiosyncratic and un-usual cut – for though he is reported to have said, in protest against the cartoonists, that his hats were made by a most reputable hatter, he is also reported to have arrived at a country house in Sussex, in the early years of motoring, 'in a little close-fitting fur-collared jacket, tight leggings and gaiters, and a little round hat which, with his half-mischievous face, made him look the exact figure of Puck'; talk, too, prolonged far into the night between days of heavy work – and even, perhaps, the pleasure, unhappily not common amongst eminent men, but which he still enjoys, of sitting in a bathing suit on the beach and singing, in company with a friend hardly less eminent than himself, the music-hall songs of happier days. To this many-sided man

No sound is dissonant that tells of life;

and for that reason he has been more hated than men of less vivid personality by his political enemies, and for that reason, too, when his hour came, at last, in 1940, he won not only the confidence of his fellow countrymen but their devoted loyalty and affection. Like Nelson, he had their hearts.

On the death of King Edward VII in 1910 the international horizon began swiftly to darken. In the following year the Kaiser sent his gunboat *Panther* to the Moroccan port of Agadir. It was a gesture only, but a significant and menacing one, for by it French claims in North Africa were openly challenged. The spectre of a German war was no new thing in the minds of French and British statesmen, but the incident at Agadir brought it suddenly and alarmingly near. The effect of it in England was very different from what the Germans had hoped; for the pacific policy of Lloyd George and the Radicals – Lloyd George had violently opposed the war in South Africa – had led them to expect that England would keep out of any war which Germany might force upon Europe. Lloyd George, however, at once disillusioned them. 'If', he declared in a speech in the City, 'a situation were to be forced upon us in which peace can only be preserved by the surrender of the great and beneficent position Britain has won by centuries of heroism and achievement, then I say emphatically that peace at that price would be a humiliation intolerable for a great country like ours to endure.' The effect upon Churchill was no less decisive. Since he left the Colonial Office his attention had been occupied by home affairs; only recently he had been opposing in Parliament McKenna's demands for an increase in naval expenditure; now, with characteristic suddenness and energy, he turned his thoughts wholly to the new danger from abroad. As Home Secretary his power to act was at the moment limited; he could, however, advise. It had always been his custom to give his views in writing upon current problems to the heads of other departments than his own – Sir Edward Grey once said, in semi-humorous resignation, that sheer activity of mind would soon make him unfit for any post in the Cabinet but that of Prime Minister; so now he sent Asquith a memorandum upon 'Military Aspects of the

Continental Problem'. Presently he was asked to attend a meeting of the Committee of Imperial Defence, to discuss strategy should war occur. The view he expressed was clear and vigorous – and contained, incidentally, a strangely accurate prophecy of what actually happened in 1914. There was, however, disagreement of a serious kind between the army and navy chiefs, and it was soon apparent that McKenna, the First Lord of the Admiralty, would have to be replaced. His most likely successor seemed to be Lord Haldane, who had brought to a successful conclusion his five years' task of reorganizing and re-equipping the army, and was eminently capable of performing a similar service for the navy. But that autumn Churchill received an invitation from Asquith to stay with him in Scotland. The two played golf together, and suddenly one afternoon, on their way home from the links, the Prime Minister asked his guest if he would like to go to the Admiralty. 'Indeed I would,' was the immediate answer. Lord Haldane, after some preliminary hesitation, accepted his friend's appointment with the best possible grace, and they worked together in harmony during the three ensuing years before war was declared.

This was the greatest opportunity which Sir Winston Churchill had yet had, and he flung himself into his new task with unsparing energy. He was happy; life, as one friend put it, melted in his mouth like butter. Gone was all thought of naval economy now; the navy was his child. That war was coming, he was convinced; and, however soon it came, the navy must be prepared. He worked to impart to everyone about him an ever-present sense of danger. He transferred his office to the Admiralty yacht and was aboard her continually. 'Who would not work', he would say, 'for such a Service?' Old Lord Fisher gave his 'beloved Winston' the benefit of his long experience; the Board of Admiralty was reconstituted;

Jellicoe was given the command of the Home Fleet, and
Beatty – later to command the Battle-cruiser Squadron –
was made the First Lord's Naval Secretary. Technical
problems were of absorbing interest: the conversion of
warships for the use of oil-fuel, the development of sub-
marines, and – in particular – the inauguration of a
naval air service. It was to Sir Winston Churchill more
than to anyone else that the Royal Naval Air Service
owed its beginning. His natural genius for the technics
of war had foreseen the future development of air fighting as early as 1913, when, at a time when most people
in England had never even seen an aeroplane, he was
urging the use of them for observation as an aid to
coastal defence. Often, during that year, he was himself
flying at Calshot on Southampton Water. By the time
of the naval review in 1914 there were a hundred aero-
planes ready for service with the fleet. Developments and
innovations in the navy cost money, and the Cabinet was
divided over the naval estimates for 1914. In the Commons Churchill – the brilliant and successful renegade
– was more hated than ever by the Conservatives. But he
got his way over the estimates, the work went on, and
the navy, when the crisis came, was ready.

The troubles in Ireland, which had boiled up at the
imminence of a Home Rule Bill into a threat of force by
the Ulstermen, receded suddenly into the background
under the fierce light of a new and more universal danger.
The Austrian Archduke was murdered at Sarajevo. A
month later the Austrians sent an ultimatum to Belgrade.
War between Austria and Serbia would be sure to involve Russia, as protector of the Slavs and competitor
with Austria for influence in the Balkans; if Russia
fought, Germany would come in against her, and Germany in the field would be bound to involve France.
General war was certain. As late as August 1st British
opinion was divided, all the Liberal newspapers de-

nouncing the idea of participating in the war. Asquith failed to carry the Cabinet with him in his plea that Britain must fight in fulfilment of her previous verbal pledge to France, and brought them round (with the exception of Morley and Burns, who resigned) only by bringing in the issue of Belgian neutrality – though there was nothing in the text of the neutrality treaties affecting Belgium which made it obligatory upon Britain to go to war for a breach of them. But events pressed; Grey sent his ultimatum to Berlin, and at 11 p.m. on the 4th of August we were at war.

It is characteristic of Sir Winston Churchill that throughout the critical days which preceded the outbreak of war, his spirits were not depressed but exalted at the prospect of the test which was to come. To Grey the thought of war was only darkness and calamity; but Grey, a great public servant who performed his onerous task only because it was his duty to do so, had his heart elsewhere – perhaps with the birds and squirrels at Falloden or with Wordsworth brooding on the

> Heavy and the weary weight
> Of all this unintelligible world;

Churchill's mind, on the contrary, though it has as many facets as a cut diamond, has never been divided – which is one secret of his power. It was not divided now; he was 'in tearing spirits' (as Asquith observed) 'at the prospect of a war'. He was still young – not quite forty; by upbringing and natural bent war was the thing he understood better than anything else, and much better than any of his colleagues did; and he was at the head of the fighting force upon which England's safety wholly depended. It was the highest adventure which, in an adventurous life, had yet confronted him.

The adventure began well. Arrangements were made for ferrying the Expeditionary Force across the Channel, and the navy successfully undertook the double duty of transporting them and of defending the country from invasion. In the autumn, things began to go badly on the Continent; the first forward rush of the Germans had been checked and the line stabilized on the Aisne, but in October Antwerp was threatened, and the loss of Antwerp would mean a German drive for the Channel ports. The Belgians were unwilling to hold it, and in conference with Kitchener and Grey Churchill proposed offering reinforcements in the hope of persuading them to hold out a few days longer. A telegram was sent, and almost immediately Churchill followed it in person. Arrived at Antwerp, he found the raw troops of the Royal Naval Division hard pressed. The Belgians agreed to postpone withdrawal for three days, but the position was critical. Once on the scene of action Churchill was unwilling to leave it, and offered to resign from the Admiralty and take command at Antwerp. The offer was refused, though Kitchener was in favour of accepting it. German pressure increased and, when the three days were up, all agreed that the town must be abandoned.

This incident did Sir Winston no good at home. The true effect of isolated actions are seldom at once apparent in war. The defence of Antwerp looked like failure – and why had the First Lord of the Admiralty left his office to participate in it? Always brilliant, always enterprising, was he also always sound? And why had the German North Sea fleet not been brought to action, or the shelling of Scarborough avenged? Such questions were easy to ask; but later historians of the war have concluded that the brief check at Antwerp to the German advance was just enough to turn the scale against them and stop their second attempt to gain a decision in the West. In the following year another unsuccessful venture in which Churchill was deeply engaged further impaired the public's confidence in him. The entry of Turkey into the war seriously affected the position of the Russians, who were fighting on the eastern front in isolation from their allies. The western front was at the moment more or less static. If the Dardanelles could be forced, the Russian Black Sea ports would be opened to British shipping with munitions for Russia; a possible Turkish attack upon Egypt would be prevented, and the Balkan States neutralized – or perhaps induced to join the Allies. The scheme was brilliant and strategically sound and Churchill worked upon it with characteristic vehemence and energy; unhappily, however, conflicting opinions upon the nature of the forces needed to carry out the enterprise delayed it until it was too late, so that when, after an unsuccessful effort to force the Narrows by ships alone, General Sir Ian Hamilton was sent out to land troops at Cape Helles, the Turks were ready for them. The landing from the *River Clyde* of the 1st Munster Fusiliers and certain companies of the 2nd Hampshires and Dublin Fusiliers, and of the Australians and New Zealanders at Anzac Cove, was one of the most gallant, and one of the most futile, operations of British military history. Less than a year later the campaign was abandoned. 'If there were any operations', Churchill said, 'in the history of the world which, having been begun, it was worth while to carry through with the utmost vigour and fury,' it was the operations in Gallipoli. He was right; but they were not carried through with vigour and fury; they were regarded at home as a mere side-show. Subsequent opinions have been expressed that, if the Dardanelles campaign had been carried out according to its original conception – which was largely Churchill's – the war could have been won in 1916.

In May 1915, barely a month after the landings at Cape Helles, Lord Fisher resigned his office of First Sea Lord, and the Conservative opposition, led by Bonar Law, demanded the resignation of Churchill as well.

Asquith consented to form a Coalition Government, and the only means of ensuring its smooth running seemed to be to let the Conservatives have their way with Churchill. He was told, therefore, that he would have to go. The only member of the Conservative party to plead for his retention was Lord Beaverbrook (as he now is). It was a cruel blow, softened a little only by warm tributes from Sir Arthur Wilson, who succeeded Fisher as First Sea Lord, and from Kitchener. 'One thing at any rate', Kitchener said, 'they cannot take from you. The fleet was ready.'

He still remained in the Cabinet as Chäncellor of the Duchy of Lancaster and still sat on the Dardanelles Committee; but when, towards the end of 1915, the campaign already looked like being abandoned, he felt that there was nothing more for him to do in London. Accordingly he applied to Asquith for a military command in France, and saw some months of service in the trenches as Colonel of the 6th Royal Scots Fusiliers. It is said that a general once, on a tour of inspection, remarked that Colonel Churchill's headquarters were fixed in a very dangerous position. 'Yes, sir,' was the answer, 'but after all this is a very dangerous war.' The amalgamation of his battalion with another unit deprived him of his command early in the following year, and he returned to England. On the fall of Asquith's government in December and the formation of the second Coalition under Lloyd George, he was offered, in spite of the violent opposition of Lord Northcliffe and the Conservatives, the post of Minister of Munitions. It was something to be in office again; but he was not a member of the War Cabinet, and was therefore excluded from the work he was best fitted to do. Not allowed to make the plans, as he afterwards wrote, he was set to make the weapons. Nevertheless, though he could not make the plans, he was still anxious to propose them, and he continued his old habit of writing memoranda on various aspects of how things should be done. During the latter part of 1917 and the early months of 1918, he was often in France, visiting the French and British lines, talking with Clemenceau (an old man after his own heart) and doing munitions business in Paris. Once the engine of his aeroplane cut out over the Channel; asked afterwards by a friend if he was afraid of dying, 'No,' he answered; 'I love life, but I don't fear death.' It was the Happy Warrior's true response to the challenge of danger.

During the war he had suffered much personal frustration, and at the end of it his name was in partial eclipse; yet by his work the fleet, when war began, was ready; the most imaginative and brilliant strategical conception of the war had been almost wholly his; to him the Air Force owed its inception, and the invention and rapid development of tanks, the decisive weapon in the final stages of the fighting, were due to him more than to any other single man. In war Sir Winston Churchill has always seen the future in the instant: as Minister of Munitions in 1918 he was ready, in the event of the war continuing for another year, to put a mechanized army into the field. No wonder he had complained to Asquith of the practice of giving high army commands to 'dug-out trash', men who apparently supposed that the tactics which succeeded at Omdurman would be equally successful at Cambrai.

In January 1919 Churchill was transferred to the War Office and was at once occupied with the difficult problems of demobilization. Immediately after the conclusion of the armistice he had urged Lloyd George to send food-ships to Hamburg. Political motives are seldom simple, and one reason for this humane proposal was the fear of revolution in a hungry Germany. What had happened in Russia might happen elsewhere, and the Russians were already preaching world revolution.

The same reason led him to support to the best of his ability the Government's half-hearted policy – for which he was not originally responsible – of sending help to the White Russians under Koltchak and Denikin. Moreover, he could not but be aware that the collapse of the Russian armies during the war, and the consequent emergence of Bolshevism, might have been prevented, if the Dardanelles campaign had been brought to a successful end. But the resistance of the White Russians to the rising tide of Bolshevism was ineffective and brief; the British and the French withdrew their support, and the Red armies carried all before them. England was sick of fighting, and it seemed to many Englishmen that Churchill had merely wished to prolong the war. His name, in those days, was not beloved; nor was his position improved when in 1922, as Home Secretary, his name came to be particularly, though unjustifiably, associated in the public mind with the chance of renewed war against Turkey. The incident of Mustapha Kemal's threat to the British troops at Chanak, though it came to nothing, hastened the fall of Lloyd George's Coalition Government. In the general election which followed Churchill was defeated at Dundee, and found himself out of Parliament for the first time for twenty-two years. The enforced leisure of the ensuing year he employed in writing the first two volumes of his *World Crisis*.

The inter-war period was amongst the most ignoble in English history. The mood of exalted idealism in which England had entered the war evaporated as it dragged on, and was succeeded by disillusionment, profound and bitter in some minds – like C. E. Montague's for instance – shallow and cynical in others. All the old certainties were gone. Cultivated society, bent upon amusement but incapable of gaiety, took Mr Aldous Huxley (then unregenerate) as its interpreter, or D. H. Lawrence whose tormented egotists' dream it preferred to the thin scientific utopias of H. G. Wells. To profess pacifism became not only safe but popular; but it was a negative pacifism, based upon disgust. Outside England, the one positive force was Communism, and towards Communism the young intellectuals (and poets) soon began to turn. In 1923 the future seemed to hold little promise for Sir Winston Churchill. Nobody wanted him. He was brilliant, but dangerous. He was a man of action, and men of action were at a discount in 1923. Moreover, he was not in Parliament, and how he could re-enter it was by no means clear. As a party man his position was dubious: nominally he was still a Coalition Liberal, but the coalition had ceased to exist, and there was no place for him with the independent Liberals under the leadership of Asquith. His experience during the year, especially as Minister of Munitions, had cooled his sympathy with the more radical element in Liberal thought, and Labour, now becoming rapidly more powerful, was bringing nearer the menace of Socialism. It was beginning to look as if he would have to return to the Conservatives. In this there was no inconsistency; for to support measures for the broadening of privilege and the relief of distress within a settled society is a different thing from supporting similar social causes when their triumph would lead to the disintegration of society itself – and to Churchill the disintegration of society was precisely what Socialism appeared to be. It was, quite simply, the abyss. The fact that in 1953 the Conservative party under Sir Winston Churchill's leadership was in agreement with the Socialist opposition over nine-tenths of its policy both domestic and foreign is one more proof, if proof were needed, of the essential stability of British institutions – and of the good sense of both parties in continuing to recognize that politics is merely 'the art of the possible'.

Early in 1924, after the general election which brought Labour into power with Liberal support, Churchill fought a by-election in the Abbey Division of Westminster as an Independent Anti-Socialist, and was defeated by forty-three votes; the following autumn, standing as a Constitutionalist for Epping, he was elected. He had already offered to cooperate with the Conservatives, and when Stanley Baldwin formed his government, he made Churchill Chancellor of the Exchequer. He was back in office again – in his father's party, and in his father's post – and remained there until 1929, when Labour was brought back to power. His five budgets were not particularly memorable, nor does one expect to find in finance a happy field for Sir Winston's qualities; there was one incident, however, during his Chancellorship, which was highly characteristic and gave him great satisfaction. During the general strike in 1926, one of the most disconcerting things for the public was the absence of news. Newspapers had ceased to appear, and the B.B.C. had not yet sufficiently grown to take their place. Under these circumstances the Government had the notion of improvising an official journal. It was done, and Churchill was appointed editor. The *British Gazette* pouring under his editorial control from the presses of the *Morning Post*, was, for a time, almost the only newspaper in the country. It did good service, and one cannot doubt that its editor enjoyed himself. The experience was 'fun' – like that other experience fifteen years before, when, as Home Secretary, Churchill had left his office to watch policemen and a company of Scots Guards besieging some armed anarchists in a house in Sidney Street. 'Now don't be cross,' he had said to a colleague on that occasion, 'it was such fun.'

For the next ten years Britain's role in world affairs was not a distinguished one. Churchill, though in Parliament, was not in office, and had no power beyond words and warnings to check the swiftly accelerating drift towards disaster. He was almost alone in his vision of the shape of what was to come, and he saw it with extraordinary clarity. As early as 1930 he painted a grim picture of England's weakness: 'The grand and victorious summits', he said in his Romanes lecture, 'which we won in the war are being lost, have indeed largely been lost in the years which followed the peace. We see our race doubtful of its mission and no longer confident about its principles, infirm of purpose, drifting to and fro with the tides and currents of a deeply-disturbed ocean.' By 1932, when the majority of Englishmen had hardly heard the name of Hitler, Churchill described him as 'the moving impulse behind the German Government', adding that 'he may be more than that very soon'. Meanwhile he was urging the redress of Germany's just grievances under the peace treaties, in the hope of preventing her from taking the law into her own hands, as he knew she would. Nobody heeded him. In 1933 Hitler seized power. Churchill's plea to make collective use of the League of Nations again fell upon deaf ears. The menace from Germany swiftly grew – and England was weak. Churchill spoke no more of redress of grievances: it was time to look to defence. With unerring foresight he called for the doubling, and redoubling of our air force, and for a combined Ministry of Defence. Again he was ignored. In 1936 Germany, in violation of the treaties, reoccupied the Rhineland, and Italy defied the League by her action in Abyssinia. Churchill confronted Baldwin with the frightful deficiencies of the British air defences, but got no reply – until suddenly Baldwin confessed that at the general election the previous year he had not dared to go to the country with a policy of rearmament – for, if he had, he would not have been returned to power. Sir Winston Churchill's lonely battle continued: faithful to principle but plastic in expedients, he urged friendship with Russia as an anti-German power, and was ready to support any political party which could see the true state of world affairs. But none did. In 1937 Chamberlain succeeded Baldwin, and the following spring Austria was annexed. Then, in the autumn, came the threat to Czechoslovakia, and Chamberlain's visit to Berchtesgaden, convinced that straight talk, as between one honest man and another, was the way to deal with dictators. Sir Winston knew better, but he was the only man who had not willed himself into blindness, and still his warnings went unregarded. 'I have watched this famous island', he said, 'descending incontinently, fecklessly, the stairway which leads to a dark gulf. It is a fine broad stairway at the beginning, but after a bit the carpet ends. A little farther on there are only flagstones, and a little farther on still these break beneath your feet.' Chamberlain flew to Munich, and returned with his famous promise – 'Peace for our time' – and England believed that the promise would be fulfilled. Churchill's wry comment was that the German dictator, instead of snatching the victuals from the table, was content to have them served to him course by course. 'By this time next year,' he said in the late autumn of 1938, 'we shall know whether the policy of appeasement has appeased, or whether it has only stimulated a more ferocious appetite.' Indeed, he knew well enough already, and before the twelve months were out England and the world knew too.

On the outbreak of war, Chamberlain, partly in submission to popular demand, called Churchill to the Admiralty; and nine months later, after the defeat of the Government in the debate on Norway, in which Churchill pointed out that the failure of Allied troops to maintain a foothold was due solely to our failure during the past five years to regain air parity with Germany,

Chamberlain resigned. He had only one possible successor; and on the very day that the Germans opened their attack upon Western Europe, Winston Churchill became Prime Minister.

England, unled for twenty years, at last found the leader whom she desperately needed. With the magnanimity which has never failed him, Churchill wasted neither time nor words in reproaches about the past: 'The time to be frightened is when evils can be remedied; when they cannot be remedied, they must be faced with courage.' Nobody noted 'tearing spirits' in him now, as on that August day a quarter of a century before: he knew too well what was in store for the country he loved. He knew, too, as he has always known, the true temper of his fellow-countrymen, that the British people once the danger is upon them have no need to be hoodwinked into courage. 'I have nothing to offer but blood, toil, tears, and sweat. . . .' Garibaldi's famous words he made his own, rightly confident that the country would respond to them. 'You ask, What is our aim? I can answer in one word: "Victory" – victory at all costs, victory in spite of all terror, victory, however long and hard the road may be; for without victory there is no survival.' The issue at stake was as simple as it was terrible, and England accepted it.

From the first moment that Winston Churchill assumed direction of the war, he had the entire confidence of the country; very soon he was to have its love as well. Men trusted him for his superb competence and courage; they loved him for qualities which, in a pre-eminent degree, he shared with themselves and which made him not only a leader but an emblem of England at war: the *gaminerie* (noted so long before by his friend Blunt), which gave a schoolboy relish to his descriptions of Mussolini – the 'tattered lackey', the 'little jackal trotting hopefully and hungrily' at Hitler's side – his contemptuous mispronunciation (so unlike the B.B.C.'s) of German names; his swift and generous recognition of others' courage, and sympathy with their suffering – interviewed by the American journalist Dorothy Thompson during the first blitz on London, he spoke to her with passionate emotion of the Londoners: 'They deserve victory,' he said, 'and by God they shall have it.' In Bristol once, he was seen standing amongst the ruins of a raid with the tears running down his face. 'We may show mercy,' he once said; 'we shall ask for none.' In all his utterances he was the voice of inarticulate England, the expression of her anger and pity, of her grim and characteristic irony, of her stubborn will to survive. England has always been lucky in her hour of need; more than once she has been brought by her fools near to the edge of the abyss and rescued by her heroes; she was never luckier than in September 1939. 'My lord,' said Chatham in an earlier crisis of English history, 'I am sure that I can save this country, and that nobody else can.' Winston Churchill might have said the same; but he did not say it: he had no need, for England said it for him.

There is not space here to follow the course of the war in detail. Many books have been written about it, and the best and fullest of them is Churchill's own work in six large volumes. But something must be said about the vision and quality of Churchill's leadership. A Greek philosopher once said that happiness consisted in activity along the lines of excellence; if that is true, as it surely is, then Churchill during the long years of war, for all their misery, was a happy man. He had found his destiny, and the work that he was meant to do. The power which he concentrated in his own hands was unprecedented in British history: dominating the War Cabinet of five members (latterly increased to seven), who were responsible for all major decisions in the conduct of the war, he was also Defence Minister, in which capacity the Chiefs of Staff reported directly to him instead of to their own Ministers; further, the Joint Planning Committee, professional staff officers of the Army, Navy, and Air Force worked under him as Minister of Defence. Thus his power was virtually absolute; it was as great as Hitler's in Germany – but with the difference that it depended upon Parliament; and Parliament, fortunately, had the sense to grant it without question, for in the early years of the war, at any rate, Churchill was the leader of a completely united nation.

In the 1914 war the big military decisions had been left to the generals; now this was no longer the case. From the beginning Churchill took absolute control of the military machine, directing not only all major questions of strategy but pressing his advice upon a host of minor matters such as under any other leader would have been delegated to subordinates. The pressure of work was enormous; few men could have supported it, but Churchill throve upon it. He had the knowledge of the expert – of the expert in many fields – and the passion of the inspired leader of men. The British are a dogged and courageous people, but, for the most part, inarticulate. During the darkest days of the war Churchill spoke not only to them, but for them. He was the voice of England, and that voice was heard across the world. 'We shall go on to the end,' he said in June 1940, when the German armies were sweeping across France; 'we shall fight on the seas and the oceans, we shall fight with growing confidence and growing strength in the air, we shall defend our island, whatever the cost may be; we shall fight on the beaches, we shall fight on the landing grounds, we shall fight in the fields and the streets, we shall fight in the hills; we shall never surrender, and even if – which I do not for a moment believe – this island were subjugated and starving, then our Empire, armed and guarded by the British Fleet, would carry on the struggle until in God's good time the new world, with all its power and might, steps forth to the rescue and liberation of the World.'

When Russia was invaded by Germany in the summer of 1941, Churchill immediately offered British support. To some this came as a surprise, as ever since the Russian revolution Churchill had been amongst the fiercest enemies of Communism. Its inhumanity, its tyranny, its atheism were opposed to everything he most valued in politics and human life. Nevertheless his decision to give Russia all possible help in her struggle with Nazi Germany was instant and inevitable. 'I have only one purpose,' he said, 'the destruction of Hitler, and my life is much simplified thereby. If Hitler invaded Hell, I would make at least a favourable reference to the Devil in the House of Commons.' The following year he visited Stalin in Moscow, and took his measure. While the war should last, Britain and Russia were allies, but Churchill was under no illusion about the nature of the alliance; apart from its immediate object, the defeat of Hitler, it was built upon sand, and Churchill was already aware of the dangers which would threaten once that object had been attained. He knew that Russia, when Germany was beaten, would be the dominant power on the Continent, and he knew what that would mean. In Churchill's view, there was only one way by which, after the war, the principles of the Atlantic Charter could be upheld and the spread of Communism checked, and that was by the closest possible association of the British Commonwealth and America. Towards this end he worked constantly; it was the basis of his whole conception of the post-war world. 'This gift of a common tongue,' he said in a speech to Harvard University, 'is a priceless inheritance, and it may well some day become the foundation of a common citizenship. I like to think of British and

Americans moving freely over each other's wide estates with hardly a sense of being foreigners to one another.'

Unfortunately, however, President Roosevelt, in spite of his close personal friendship with Churchill, did not share these ideas. Roosevelt admired Britain, but he was suspicious of British imperialism. He thought that the danger to the Atlantic Charter (the independence of small nations; the upholding of the rights of Man; the spreading of free institutions) would come not from Russian ambition but from British and French colonialism. Churchill, during their many meetings during the course of the war, tried to persuade him otherwise, but without success. Roosevelt, indeed, hardened in his animosity to British colonialism, an animosity which was, moreover, deeply ingrained in the American mind. One of the results of this was that Roosevelt's attitude towards Russia became more and more tolerant and even credulous. He refused to believe in the Russian design for the spread of world Communism after the war. 'I have a hunch,' he said, 'that Stalin doesn't want anything but security for his country; he will work for a world of democracy and peace.' Other high American officials shared the President's view. 'The Russians,' wrote Harry Hopkins, 'trust the United States more than they trust any other power in the world; they want to maintain friendly relations with us; they are a determined people who think and act just like we do.' It is easy to be wise after the event; but Churchill was wise before it: he knew perfectly well that Russian Communism was bent upon capturing the world, and that the ideas upon which it was based would – given the chance – destroy utterly everything which was most precious in the life of Western civilization.

The depth of the division between his own and the American way of thinking was not apparent to Churchill until the Teheran Conference, when he, Roosevelt, and

Stalin met together for the first time. To Churchill it was bitter, for he loved and admired Roosevelt as much as any man in the world. After Roosevelt's generous offer of support through 'lend-lease' before America entered the war, Churchill had called him the best friend England had ever had, and with characteristic loyalty he would never afterwards allow a derogatory word to be spoken of him in his presence. But the division was there, and it went to the root of Churchill's design for the close cooperation of America and the British Commonwealth as the one defence in the post-war years against Russian imperialism.

At Teheran, in December 1943, Stalin, Roosevelt, and Churchill agreed upon the grand strategy which was to end the war: the invasion of Normandy across the Channel, the blow at Southern France through Italy, and the Russian offensive on the Eastern front. Churchill pressed for a further operation in the Eastern Mediterranean, by which Turkey might be brought in on the allied side and the Black Sea opened up; but Roosevelt was adamant against it, suspecting a selfish motive in the extension of British influence in the Balkans. The plan was therefore dropped. From that time onward Churchill knew that anything which could be done to check the spread of Russian domination in Europe after the war would have to be done by himself alone, without the support of Roosevelt and the United States. Hence he further urged that the Western armies in their final offensives should liberate Prague and, especially, Berlin and any other key territories the possession of which would, after the war, strengthen their hands to force Russia to keep the pledges she had made at the Yalta Conference to maintain the independence of small nations. But here again Churchill was unable to carry his point, though he continued to press it with all the force he could command upon Roosevelt's successor,

President Truman. For the American leaders the destruction of the German armies was the only objective; Churchill's foresight as to the political dangers from Russia once the war was won they brushed aside as selfish and irrelevant. Had they listened to him, many of the problems and perils of the post-war world might never have arisen.

At the end of the war no statesman had ever stood higher than Churchill in the affections and esteem not only of his country but of the whole Western world. Yet in the General Election of 1945, a few weeks after Germany's surrender, he and his party were defeated by an overwhelming majority. Once again Britain chose to dispense with Churchill's services. It was a bitter blow to him. 'I had acquired', he wrote, 'the chief power in the State, which henceforth I wielded in ever-growing measure for five years and three months of world war, at the end of which time, all our enemies having surrendered unconditionally or being about to do so, I was immediately dismissed by the British electorate from all further conduct of their affairs.' To Churchill it looked like ingratitude; yet he knew as well as anyone that there is no sentiment in politics: they are a practical business, and the fact is that Britain as a whole wanted a programme of far-reaching social reform such as only the Labour Party seemed to offer. Many of Churchill's friends urged him to leave politics; but he had no intention of doing so. For so many years politics had been the breath of life to him; he could not forgo it. 'I am a child', he said, 'of the House of Commons.' As Leader of the Opposition he flung himself into his work not, perhaps, with characteristic wisdom but certainly with characteristic vigour. 'The Socialist belief', he declared, 'is that nothing matters so long as miseries are equally shared, and certainly the Socialists have acted in accordance with their faith.' In his speeches in the House and elsewhere he prophesied bankruptcy and every sort of disaster as the result of Socialist rule; but this time his prophecies were not to be fulfilled. The virulence of his opposition was due partly, perhaps, to his long love of the rough and tumble of debate, partly to the fact that he was genuinely out of touch with home affairs after the period in which he had been exclusively occupied with the conduct of the war. Much of his energy was, however, still directed to foreign affairs, where his truest interest had always lain. He continued passionately to advocate the closest possible ties with the United States, and to call for a united Western Europe with the pledged support of America and Britain. American trust in Russian sincerity was already weakening, and it was finally broken by Churchill's speech at Fulton in Missouri in the March of 1946. In this great speech he pleaded for the 'fraternal association of the English-speaking peoples' against the terrifying march of Communism. From then on, the association became a reality.

Meanwhile in the intervals of business Churchill was writing his *History of the Second World War*, employing an army of secretaries and dictating, as his habit is, far into the night. He bought his estate at Chartwell and began farming; he continued to paint – and wrote a book on the subject; he bought a colt, Colonist II, and went in for racing; he travelled over much of America and visited half the capitals of Europe, speaking on the great theme nearest to his heart. He was seventy-five, but the energy of youth was a perpetual fountain in him.

In 1951 Labour was defeated at the polls by a narrow margin; the Conservatives returned to power – or a semblance of power – and Churchill, now seventy-six years old, found himself for the first time Prime Minister in time of peace. In 1953 he was made Knight of the Garter. Two years later he resigned the premiership.

Can one sum up in a sentence the career of this extra-ordinarily able and versatile man? First (if one tried) would come his love of England and of all that is noblest in her history; then the determination, which lay behind all his public work, to preserve the freedoms which are essential to a Christian country. Finally, the Western world owes to him more than to any one man the bringing together, now so nearly achieved, of the British Commonwealth and the United States of America in all major problems of World politics, and the first tentative steps towards a united Europe.

Some other Puffin Books
are described on the
last few pages

THE RADIUM WOMAN

Eleanor Doorly

PS 68

The Radium Woman was Madame Curie, the great scientist who discovered radium, and this is an entrancing story of her strange experiences in Poland under the Russian Tsar – 'Born in servitude and chained in our cradles' – of gay dancing days, too, and sleigh rides; of a secret society for the patriots – and exile to the frozen plains of Siberia waiting for anyone who was found out. Paris and her University were far away but never out of mind, though the money had to be earned and there was a sister's education to be saved for first. She was always tremendously alive, and, even in the exciting days of her famous research for radium, she had also a husband and baby to love, and neglected neither.

This account of her life is inspiring and can be read simply as a magnificent story, as well as to see how a child grew to be one of the modern world's most famous scientists. It is illustrated with beautiful woodcuts by Robert Gibbings, and will appeal to boys and girls of eleven and over.

SPARE-TIME BOOKS

ENJOYING PAINTINGS · *A. C. Ward*

A book to help you look at pictures and to understand them, illustrated by many photographs of famous paintings (PS 84)

GOING INTO THE PAST · *Gordon Copley*

An introduction to the pleasures of discovery and to the means of searching for the things ancient man left behind in Britain. With 16 pages of photographs and many line illustrations (PS 117)

GOING TO A CONCERT · *Lionel Salter*

A book for people going to their first big concerts, explaining how the orchestra is made up, how a composer sets to work, and so on. With photographs of orchestras and players (PS 85)

GOING TO THE BALLET · *Arnold Haskell*

A wonderful introduction to ballet, simple but deeply informed, being written by the original 'balletomane' himself. Illustrated with many pictures (PS 86)

GOING TO THE OPERA · *Lionel Salter*

An easy book to take you inside the world of opera, and to help you enjoy more thoroughly what you hear there. Illustrated with photographs (PS 118)